MW00606257

QUICK PREP COOKING
USING INGREDIENTS FROM
TRADER JOE'S

QUICK PREP COOKING
USING INGREDIENTS FROM
TRADER JOE'S

JORDAN ZELESNICK
Creator of JZ Eats

PAGE STREET
PUBLISHING CO.

PAGE STREET
PUBLISHING CO.

Copyright © 2024 Jordan Zelesnick

First published in 2024 by
Page Street Publishing Co.
27 Congress Street, Suite 1511
Salem, MA 01970
www.pagestreetpublishing.com

All rights reserved. No part of this book may be reproduced or used, in any form or by any means, electronic or mechanical, without prior permission in writing from the publisher.

Distributed by Macmillan, sales in Canada by The Canadian Manda Group.

28   27   26   25   24   1   2   3   4   5

ISBN-13: 978-1-64567-946-2
ISBN-10: 1-64567-946-2

Library of Congress Control Number: 2023936667

Cover and book design by Meg Baskis for Page Street Publishing Co.
Photography by Katrina Akafor

Printed and bound in China

Page Street Publishing protects our planet by donating to nonprofits like The Trustees, which focuses on local land conservation.

To my husband, Shane, thank you for believing in me and pushing me to leave the corporate world to pursue my business. I was terrified and you made me believe in myself. Thank you for tasting every recipe, even the bad ones. My life has forever changed because you believed in me. I love you!

CONTENTS

INTRODUCTION

I've always had a special appreciation for food. It was by accident that I became a food blogger almost 10 years ago. At the time, it was a hobby and a passion project, and now it's my full-time job!

It was also by accident that I started an Easy Trader Joe's Meals series on Instagram and TikTok. What began as a creative outlet for me is now the opportunity of a lifetime: Getting to put all of that into a cookbook!

The popular series began when I was in the midst of wedding planning and moving to a new state where I didn't know anyone—completely stressed out, overwhelmed and stretched thin. I still wanted home-cooked meals but no longer had the time or energy to create the types of dinners I was used to.

I needed something quick and easy, that didn't lack in flavor. And that's where the Easy Trader Joe's Meals series was born. It occurred to me that there must be others in the same stressed-out, overwhelmed boat as me, so I started sharing my Trader Joe's creations in hopes of helping others. To my surprise, multiple videos went viral and my audience *loved* the series.

"I'm living for this series" . . . "This series is saving me right now, thank you!" . . . "I'm so happy I found your Trader Joe's series!" . . . My comments and DMs quickly filled up with messages just like these.

These easy Trader Joe's meals brought me back to my college days, when I would pick up various items from the frozen food section and throw them together with some fresh ingredients for an easy meal. I survived off frozen gnocchi back then! My usual way to prepare it was with pan-seared chicken or some sort of seafood, usually shrimp, and some fresh veggies. It was my favorite thing to make.

Trader Joe's salad kits and frozen foods are the perfect starting points for a quick recipe. In this book, I show you how to take those ingredients and make a delicious complete meal out of them.

NOTE: Please keep in mind that some Trader Joe's ingredients are seasonal, so make sure to snag them when you see them. If you stock up, you can make all these recipes year-round.

My goal is to provide easy and approachable dishes that taste amazing. I want you to feel that you're eating at a restaurant when you cook from my book.

You don't need fancy or expensive ingredients to create restaurant-worthy meals; it's all about knowing the right herbs and food pairings—including Trader Joe's products.

With this cookbook, I hope to give Trader Joe's-goers a full collection of recipes from boujie toasts (my favorite) to effortless dinners, where all the ingredients can be found in one store! With my cookbook, you can confidently step foot in your local Trader Joe's, assured that you will find everything you need to create any of these delicious recipes.

WEEKNIGHT WONDERS

Say goodbye to boring weeknight dinners and hello to these super simple, tasty and delicious recipes. They're perfect for busy nights when you need something delicious and hassle-free.

The goal of this chapter is to give you easy dinner recipes that can be made quickly and efficiently, without using lots of ingredients. So, many of the dishes rely on pre-prepared ingredients, such as Trader Joe's Spatchcocked Lemon Rosemary Chicken and Trader Joe's Riced Hearts of Palm, used in the recipe for Lemon Rosemary Spatchcocked Chicken and "Rice" (page 13); and the Trader Joe's Shawarma Chicken Thighs with Trader Joe's Mediterranean Style Hummus used in the Chicken Shawarma Hummus Bowls recipe (page 17).

There's nothing quite like a one-pot meal that uses few dishes and doesn't require your attention to be drawn in multiple directions. It saves time in the kitchen while ensuring you can still get something tasty on the table fast. Check out Langostino "Lobster" Rolls (page 33) or the Miso Butter Ramen (page 21) for a heart-warming noodle dish.

So, put on your comfiest sweatpants, pour yourself a glass of wine and let's whip up some easy, delicious dinners!

LEMON ROSEMARY SPATCHCOCKED CHICKEN AND "RICE"

PREP TIME: 10 minutes
COOK TIME: 1 to 1¼ hours
SERVINGS: 4

One of my favorite things about Trader Joe's is their prepared ingredients that actually taste good! Like their Spatchcocked Lemon Rosemary Chicken. It's perfectly seasoned and comes out tender and juicy every time. Here, you'll have a juicy, lemony chicken that simply roasts to perfection before being served alongside fresh veggies and Riced Hearts of Palm. This is the ideal dish for when you need something elegant on the table with little preparation and in a reasonable amount of time.

Olive oil, for cooking

1 Spatchcocked Lemon Rosemary Chicken

1 yellow onion, diced

1 zucchini (about 6 oz [170 g]), diced

Salt and freshly ground black pepper

1 tsp 21 Seasoning Salute

9 oz (255 g) Riced Hearts of Palm

Preheat the oven to 400°F (200°C) and lightly oil a shallow baking dish.

Place your spatchcocked chicken, skin side up, in the prepared baking dish and roast for 15 minutes. Then, lower the heat to 375°F (190°C) and roast for 45 to 60 minutes, or until the internal temperature of the chicken has reached 165°F (73°C).

About 15 minutes before the chicken is finished cooking, in a medium-sized skillet, heat 1 tablespoon (15 ml) of olive oil over medium-high heat. Add the onion and zucchini to the pan. Add salt and pepper to taste, plus the 21 Seasoning Salute, and sauté, stirring occasionally, for 6 to 7 minutes, or until the onion is translucent and the zucchini is tender.

Add the Riced Hearts of Palm to the pan, give them a toss and cook for 2 to 4 minutes, or until fully heated.

To serve, carve the chicken and divide the vegetable mixture and chicken among four plates.

NOTE: Even though it's already marinated, I like to season the chicken with some garlic powder, onion powder and paprika before roasting, for more flavor. The paprika will give it nice color, too.

SOYAKI CHICKEN BOWLS

PREP TIME: 15 minutes
COOK TIME: 16 to 20 minutes
SERVINGS: 4

These bowls are a vibrant and flavorful meal: First, fluffy jasmine rice is topped with a colorful array of shredded cabbage, crunchy bell peppers and meaty shiitake mushrooms. Tender shredded chicken is then smothered in the deliciously sweet and savory Soyaki Sauce, which adds a zingy kick to the dish. Thinly sliced green onions, fresh cucumber and creamy avocado provide a refreshing contrast to the rich flavors of the chicken and sauce. Finally, the dish is generously sprinkled with Trader Joe's Furikake Japanese Multi-Purpose Seasoning, which adds a satisfying crunch and a savory umami taste.

2 (10-oz [280-g]) packages Frozen Jasmine Rice

2 cups (180 g) Organic Shredded Green & Red Cabbage with Carrots

1 yellow bell pepper, seeded and ribs removed, cut into matchsticks

1 red bell pepper, seeded and ribs removed, cut into matchsticks

2 tbsp (30 ml) olive oil

8 oz (225 g) whole shiitake mushrooms

3 cooked chicken breasts, shredded

½ cup (120 ml) Soyaki Sauce

½ cup (27 g) thinly sliced green onions

1 cucumber, sliced thinly

2 avocados, peeled, pitted and sliced thinly

Furikake Japanese Multi-Purpose Seasoning

Heat the rice according to the package instructions, then set aside until you're ready to assemble the bowls.

In a large bowl, combine the cabbage and bell peppers, then set aside.

In a medium-sized skillet, heat the olive oil over medium heat. Add the mushrooms, cover and cook for 2 to 3 minutes, or until they release their juices. Remove the lid and sauté the mushrooms until golden brown, 10 to 12 minutes. Add the cabbage mixture, shredded chicken and Soyaki Sauce to the pan, toss to coat and cook for 4 to 5 minutes. Add the green onions and toss to combine.

Divide the rice among four bowls and top with the chicken mixture, sliced cucumber and avocados. Season with the furikake seasoning and serve warm.

CHICKEN SHAWARMA HUMMUS BOWLS

PREP TIME: 5 minutes
COOK TIME: 31 to 34 minutes
SERVINGS: 2

The chicken thighs in this dish will change how you feel about chicken thighs forever! I used to dislike chicken thighs, but love them now because of this recipe. They air fry to crispy perfection, making them a wonderful adornment for bowls of caramelized onions, mushrooms and creamy hummus.

1 (1½-lb [680-g]) package Shawarma Chicken Thighs

2 tbsp (28 g) unsalted butter

1½ tsp (5 ml) olive oil

2 yellow onions, sliced very thinly

15 oz (425 g) sliced shiitake mushrooms

Kosher salt

2 cloves garlic, minced

2 tbsp (30 ml) Worcestershire sauce

1½ tsp (6 g) Multipurpose Umami Seasoning Blend

½ cup (123 g) Mediterranean Style Hummus

2 tbsp (8 g) chopped fresh parsley

Preheat an air fryer to 375°F (190°C). Place the chicken thighs in a single layer in the air fryer basket and cook for 20 minutes, flipping at the 10-minute point. They will get so crispy this way! Slice the chicken into thin strips when it's finished cooking.

Meanwhile, in a large nonstick skillet, heat the butter and olive oil over medium heat, then add the onions and toss to coat. Let the onions cook undisturbed for 5 minutes before tossing again. Repeat this process until the onions are golden brown, about 15 minutes total.

When the onions have caramelized, push them to the side and add the mushrooms along with a pinch of salt. Cover and cook for 3 to 4 minutes, or until the mushrooms begin to soften. Once the mushrooms have cooked down a bit, add the garlic, Worcestershire sauce and umami seasoning. Toss to coat, then continue to cook, tossing occasionally, for 8 to 10 minutes, or until the mushrooms have reduced by about half their size and begin to brown.

To serve, layer the bowls with two heaping scoops of hummus, plus the mushrooms, caramelized onions and chicken. Garnish with fresh parsley and serve.

NOTE: I like to cook the chicken thighs in an air fryer because they get super crispy, but you can also follow the package instructions to make them in the oven.

SPICY WONTON BOWLS

PREP TIME: 5 minutes
COOK TIME: 8 to 10 minutes
SERVINGS: 2

These bowls are fresh and light with a combination of baby bok choy, wontons and an array of garnishes. The baby bok choy is cooked to perfection in sesame oil with garlic, shallot and a splash of soy sauce. The dish is elevated with the addition of Crunchy Chili Onion, which adds just the right amount of heat and crunch. Each bite is a harmony of textures and flavors, with the tender bok choy, the umami-rich sauce and the crisp green onions. Topped with sesame seeds for a little extra crunch, these bowls are a guaranteed crowd-pleaser.

1 tbsp (15 ml) sesame oil

3 cloves garlic, minced

1 large shallot, sliced

2 bunches baby bok choy, cleaned and halved

2 tbsp (30 ml) water

1 to 2 tbsp (15 to 30 ml) soy sauce

12 oz (340 g) Frozen Chicken Cilantro Mini Wontons

¼ tsp kosher salt

¼ tsp freshly ground black pepper

2 tbsp (36 g) Crunchy Chili Onion

2 green onions, sliced thinly

Sesame seeds, to garnish

In a large nonstick skillet over medium-high heat, heat the sesame oil. Add the garlic and shallot. Cook until fragrant, 30 to 60 seconds.

Place the bok choy, cut side down, in the pan and let cook undisturbed for about 1½ minutes, or until the bottom begins to turn golden brown.

Pour in the water and soy sauce, add the wontons to the pan and season with salt and pepper. Cover immediately with a tight-fitting lid. Lower the heat to medium-low and cook for 3 to 5 minutes, or until the bok choy is tender and the leaves are slightly wilted. Transfer the bok choy into two serving bowls while the wontons finish cooking, uncovered, for about 3 more minutes, or until they are fully heated through.

When the wontons are ready, transfer them to the bowls of bok choy. Top with the Crunchy Chili Onion, sliced green onions and sesame seeds.

NOTE: Give this a try with Chicken Gyoza Potstickers, too!

MISO BUTTER RAMEN

PREP TIME: 5 minutes
COOK TIME: 14 to 15 minutes
SERVINGS: 2

This isn't your ordinary instant noodle cup. It's a velvety, savory broth filled with tender noodles, smothered in creamy miso butter that melts in your mouth like a dream. The result is a mouthwatering, umami-packed experience that will have you slurping up every last noodle. It's comfort food meets gourmet, and it's everything you never knew you needed in a bowl of ramen. You can vary them with what you have on hand, too, particularly if you have veggies in your fridge that you need to use up.

2 large eggs

6 tbsp (90 ml) warm water (about 90°F [32°C])

1 tbsp (13 g) sugar

2 tbsp (30 ml) rice vinegar

¾ cup (175 ml) soy sauce

4 (1.5-oz [43-g]) packages ramen noodles

6 tbsp (85 g) unsalted butter

1 tbsp (16 g) miso paste

4 cloves garlic, diced finely

2 tbsp (36 g) Crunchy Chili Onion

¼ cup (14 g) thinly sliced green onions

Bring a small pot of water to a boil. Carefully drop in the eggs, one at a time, and cook for 7 minutes. When the eggs are finished cooking, transfer them to a bowl of ice water and let them cool for 5 minutes before peeling.

Meanwhile, in a small bowl, combine the warm water, sugar, vinegar and soy sauce. Mix until the sugar has dissolved. Place the peeled eggs in the soy sauce mixture, making sure they are fully submerged, to marinate while you prepare the ramen. You can use a ziplock bag for this step, if you prefer.

To make the ramen, bring a large pot of water to a rolling boil. Once boiling, add the ramen noodles and cook for 5 to 6 minutes, or until al dente.

While the ramen is cooking, melt the butter in a skillet over medium heat. Then, add the miso paste and garlic; whisking until fully combined with the butter.

When the noodles are ready, drain and transfer them to the garlic miso butter and toss to coat.

To serve, divide the noodles between two bowls, and top with Crunchy Chili Onion and sliced green onions.

SPICY CREAMY TOMATO NOODLES

PREP TIME: 5 minutes
COOK TIME: 20 minutes
SERVINGS: 4

Looking for a quick and easy meal that packs a punch? Look no further than these squiggly noodles, which are coated in a fiery tomato sauce made with soy sauce and Trader Joe's Crunchy Chili Onion for an extra kick. And let's not forget the creamy factor—the whole milk and Parmesan cheese make for a velvety finish. Top it all off with some fresh basil, and you've got a dish that's sure to spice up any mealtime. No matter when you're serving up these noodles, they're guaranteed to please.

2 tbsp (30 ml) olive oil

1 white onion, sliced very thinly

Pinch of kosher salt

4 (3.25-oz [91-g]) packages Squiggly Knife Cut Style Noodles

5 oz (140 g) tomato paste

2 tbsp (30 ml) soy sauce

2 tbsp (36 g) Crunchy Chili Onion

¾ cup (175 ml) whole milk

2 tbsp (10 g) grated Parmesan cheese, for garnish

3 tbsp (9 g) chopped fresh basil, for garnish

Bring a large pot of salted water to a boil.

Meanwhile, in a large skillet, heat the olive oil over medium-high heat. Add the onion and a pinch of salt, and cook for 2 minutes, stirring frequently, then lower the heat to medium and cook for 10 minutes, or until soft and starting to brown.

When the water is boiling, add the noodles to the pot and cook until al dente, about 5 minutes. Quickly drain, reserving 1 cup (240 ml) of the pasta water.

When the onion has softened, increase the heat to medium-high. Then, add the tomato paste, soy sauce and Crunchy Chili Onion. Stir constantly for 1 minute, until the mixture is combined and the tomato paste darkens.

Add ½ cup (120 ml) of the reserved pasta water and the milk to the tomato mixture, stirring until smooth and fully combined, adding more pasta water if necessary. Bring to a light simmer, then remove from the heat and add the cooked noodles, tossing with the sauce until they are fully coated. Serve garnished with Parmesan cheese and basil.

NOTE: Make this dish healthier by using the Trader Joe's Hearts of Palm Pasta!

BUFFALO CHICKEN STUFFED PEPPERS

PREP TIME: 15 minutes
COOK TIME: 4 hours 30 minutes
SERVINGS: 8

Stuffed peppers are a delicious classic, but whew, these are really something special: tender chicken doused in tangy Buffalo sauce, mixed with creamy cheese and stuffed into colorful bell peppers. It's like a party in your mouth and everyone's invited! Whether you're looking for something to serve as a game day snack or a quick and easy healthy dinner, these stuffed peppers are sure to satisfy your hunger and your taste buds.

---

2 boneless, skinless chicken breasts

1 small yellow onion, diced

¾ cup (175 ml) hot sauce

2 tbsp (28 g) unsalted butter

1 tbsp (15 ml) honey

4 large bell peppers

½ cup (115 g) Greek yogurt

¾ cup (113 g) shredded mozzarella cheese

¼ cup (14 g) thinly sliced green onions, for garnish

In the bowl of a slow cooker, combine both chicken breasts with the onion, hot sauce, butter and honey (which will form your Buffalo sauce). Cook on LOW for 4 hours.

Meanwhile, slice the bell peppers in half from the top down and remove the seeds and ribs.

When the chicken is finished cooking, transfer it to a plate and shred with two forks. Place the shredded chicken back in the slow cooker and toss in its Buffalo sauce.

Stir in the Greek yogurt, then fold in the mozzarella cheese.

Meanwhile, about 30 minutes before the chicken is finished cooking, preheat the oven to 400°F (200°C) and arrange the bell peppers, flesh side down, in an enameled baking dish. Bake for 15 minutes, or until they begin to soften. Optional: Broil on HIGH for 1 to 2 minutes to brown the peppers.

Remove the peppers from the oven, turn them over in their pan and stuff them with the Buffalo chicken mixture. Bake the stuffed peppers for 30 to 35 minutes, or until the peppers are fork-tender.

To serve, top the stuffed peppers with the green onions.

NOTES

- I also tested this with the Trader Joe's Truffle Hot Sauce with Black Truffles and it was delicious.

- You can top them with crumbled blue cheese, too, if you like.

ZESTY LEMON PASTA WITH BALSAMIC CHICKEN

PREP TIME: 5 minutes
COOK TIME: 30 minutes
SERVINGS: 4

Swirls of thin capellini pasta, lemony sauce with red pepper flakes, Parmesan, basil and tangy balsamic chicken, oh my! There is nothing better than this elegant-looking pasta dish for a dinner for four, as it requires little effort to make while being wildly delicious.

---

4 cups (946 ml) water

¼ cup (60 ml) extra virgin olive oil

5 tbsp (71 g) unsalted butter, divided

3 cloves garlic, chopped

1 tbsp (4 g) red pepper flakes

½ tsp kosher salt

12 oz (340 g) uncooked capellini pasta

½ cup (20 g) torn fresh basil leaves, plus more for garnish

Zest and juice of 3 lemons, plus more zest for garnish

¼ cup (25 g) grated Parmesan cheese, plus more for garnish

1 (12-oz [340-g]) package Grilled Balsamic Vinegar & Rosemary Chicken, heated and sliced into 1" (2.5-cm) strips

In a medium-sized saucepan, bring the water to a boil. You might not need all of it, but it's better to have extra than not enough!

In a large nonstick skillet (large enough for your uncooked noodles to lie flat), heat the olive oil and 3 tablespoons (43 g) of the butter over medium heat.

Add the garlic, red pepper flakes and salt to the pan, and mix to combine.

Add about ½ cup (120 ml) of the boiling water to the skillet and place the pasta in the pan. Gently push the pasta around the pan with a spatula. When the water has been absorbed, add another ½ cup (120 ml) and repeat until the pasta is just about al dente.

Add the basil and the lemon zest and juice to the pan. Toss and cook for 1 to 2 more minutes.

When the pasta is ready, remove from the heat and mix in the remaining 2 tablespoons (28 g) of butter and the Parmesan cheese. To serve, divide the pasta among four plates and top with the sliced balsamic chicken. I like to garnish it with basil, lemon zest and Parmesan cheese.

NOTE: This pasta has a little bit of a kick from the red pepper flakes; if you want it to be milder, use about a teaspoon (1 g), instead of a tablespoon (4 g), of red pepper flakes.

GOCHUJANG SALMON BURGERS

PREP TIME: 20 minutes
COOK TIME: 30 minutes
SERVINGS: 10 salmon burgers

These tender salmon burgers make me salivate with their fiery gochujang, green onions and veggies, and a tangy, sweet and spicy gochujang aioli. Literally, life-changing! You can serve them on a bun or on their own with the gochujang aioli as an appetizer, or have them over rice with a steamed vegetable, such as bok choy or broccoli.

1½ lb (680 g) salmon

Kosher salt and freshly ground black pepper

1 large shallot, diced

1 red bell pepper, seeded and ribs removed, diced

¼ cup (14 g) thinly sliced green onions

2 tbsp (4 g) gochujang paste

1 tbsp (14 g) mayonnaise

2 large eggs

½ cup (30 g) panko bread crumbs

GOCHUJANG AIOLI

⅔ cup (150 g) mayonnaise

2 to 3 tbsp (40 to 60 g) gochujang paste, depending on desired level of spice

1 tbsp (15 ml) rice vinegar

2 tsp (10 ml) toasted sesame oil

2 cloves garlic, grated

½ tsp honey

¼ tsp kosher salt

TO ASSEMBLE

10 brioche buns, lightly toasted

1 to 2 (0.4-oz [11.3-g]) packages Seaweed Snacks

1 (5-oz [140-g]) bag of mixed greens or microgreens

Preheat the oven to 400°F (200°C). Place the salmon on a foil-lined baking sheet. Season the salmon with salt and pepper. Bake for 12 to 15 minutes, or until the internal temperature of the salmon reaches 135°F (57°C); it should be ever so slightly undercooked. When the salmon is done, remove from the oven and allow to cool. Remove the skin by sliding a spatula between the flesh and the skin. Transfer the salmon to a large bowl and shred with two forks.

Add the shallot, red bell pepper, green onions, gochujang paste, mayonnaise, eggs, panko bread crumbs and salt and pepper to the salmon. Mix until everything is well combined.

To make the salmon patties, preheat your broiler to HIGH and move the rack 2 to 3 inches (5 to 8 cm) from the broiler element. Using a ½-cup (4-oz [120-ml]) measuring cup per patty, form the mixture into patties on an oiled baking sheet and broil for 8 to 10 minutes, or until they begin to char.

While the salmon patties bake, prepare the gochujang aioli: In a small bowl, combine the mayonnaise, gochujang paste, vinegar, sesame oil, garlic, honey and salt and mix well.

When the salmon patties are ready, assemble your burgers: Spread an even layer of the gochujang aioli over the bottom half of each brioche bun, add two or three seaweed snacks and some mixed greens, then top with a salmon burger. Place the other half of the bun on top and serve.

SALMON RICE BOWLS

PREP TIME: 10 minutes
COOK TIME: 10 minutes
SERVINGS: 2

Luscious, tender salmon is marinated in Trader Joe's Soyaki Sauce before being cooked and served on a bed of ginger-scented rice alongside a mixture of greens, pomegranate arils and sesame seeds. The sweet and savory notes in the dish make it truly special.

1 lb (455 g) salmon, cut into 2" (50-cm) cubes

1 cup (240 ml) Soyaki Sauce, plus more for drizzling

1 (10-oz [280-g]) package Frozen Jasmine Rice

2 Frozen Ginger Cubes

¼ tsp kosher salt

1½ tsp (8 ml) extra virgin olive oil

1½ cups (83 g) mixed salad greens

½ cup (115 g) pomegranate arils

½ tsp sesame seeds

Place the cubed salmon in a shallow bowl or a gallon-sized freezer bag and add the Soyaki Sauce. Allow the salmon to marinate for 20 to 30 minutes.

Meanwhile, cook the rice according to the package instructions. Place the rice in a bowl with the ginger cubes, salt and olive oil. Cover for 2 minutes, then fluff with a fork.

When the salmon is finished marinating, drain off and discard the marinade. Heat a large nonstick skillet over medium heat. Place the marinated salmon, in a single layer, in the pan and cook for 2 to 3 minutes per side, or until fully cooked.

Divide the ginger rice between two bowls and layer with the mixed greens, cooked salmon, pomegranate arils and sesame seeds.

NOTE: The salmon skin can be left on or removed, depending on your preference.

LANGOSTINO "LOBSTER" ROLLS

PREP TIME: 5 minutes
COOK TIME: 15 minutes
SERVINGS: 2

These seem so fancy and yet are so easy! Just use some butter (lots of butter) to ensure the brioche buns become nice and golden and the langostino tails cook to tender perfection. Then, fill the buns with the langostino and top with a little fresh chives and lemon. This simple combination screams "utter perfection" and will make you feel you are by the sea!

½ cup (114 g) salted butter, divided

2 Brioche Hot Dog Buns

8 oz (225 g) frozen Langostino tails, defrosted

¼ cup (12 g) finely diced fresh chives, for garnish

2 lemon wedges, for serving

In a large skillet, melt 2 tablespoons (28 g) of the butter over medium heat. Add the buns and toast on their outsides. Transfer to a plate and set aside.

Lower the heat to medium-low and melt 3 more tablespoons (43 g) of the butter. Drain the langostino tails and dry them with a paper towel.

Add the langostino tails to the skillet and toss to coat in the butter. Heat for 2 to 3 minutes, tossing occasionally. Push the langostino tails to one side of the pan and melt the remaining 3 tablespoons (43 g) of the butter on the other side.

Brush the insides of the rolls with the melted butter, then fill them with the buttered langostino tails. Top each roll with fresh chives and serve warm with lemon wedges.

NOTE: If you don't have salted butter, add a few generous pinches of salt to the melted butter.

LANGOSTINO "FRA DIAVOLO"

PREP TIME: 10 minutes
COOK TIME: 18 to 28 minutes
SERVINGS: 4

With its fiery red sauce and succulent Langostino, this is a seafood lover's dream. And unlike its pricey cousin, lobster Fra Diavolo, it won't pinch your wallet too hard. So, spice up your fancy date night pasta with this affordable and easy-to-make version of the classic Italian dish.

1 tbsp (15 ml) extra virgin olive oil

5 cloves garlic, minced

1 shallot, diced

2 tsp (3 g) crushed red pepper flakes

1 tsp dried oregano

¼ cup (60 ml) white cooking wine

2 tbsp (32 g) tomato paste

1 (28-oz [800-g]) can crushed tomatoes with juices

8 Campari tomatoes, quartered

1 bay leaf

Kosher salt and freshly ground black pepper

1 lb (455 g) uncooked spaghetti

12 oz (340 g) frozen Langostino tails, defrosted

3 tbsp (9 g) chopped fresh basil, plus more for serving

3 tbsp (12 g) chopped fresh parsley, plus more for serving

Bring a large pot of salted water to a boil.

In a large skillet, heat the olive oil and sauté the garlic and shallot until fragrant and slightly translucent, about 2 minutes. Then, add the red pepper flakes, oregano and cooking wine, while scraping the bottom of the pan with a wooden spoon to remove any browned bits. Let simmer until reduced by half, then add the tomato paste, crushed tomatoes and their juices, Campari tomatoes, bay leaf and salt and pepper to taste. Simmer for 5 to 10 minutes, stirring occasionally, while the pasta is cooking.

Add the spaghetti to the boiling water and cook for 8 to 12 minutes, or until al dente.

When the pasta is ready, reserve ¼ cup (60 ml) of the pasta water, drain and add the pasta to the pan of sauce. Add the langostino tails, basil and parsley, tossing everything together to fully coat the pasta and langostino tails. Mix in the pasta water and simmer for 3 to 4 minutes to heat the langostino tails, tossing occasionally.

Remove the bay leaf before serving and garnish with more fresh herbs.

MODERN STEAK AND TATERS

PREP TIME: 5 minutes

COOK TIME: 25 to 30 minutes

SERVINGS: 2

Give me steak and potatoes, and I'm there! Steak and potatoes are delicious in all forms, but this version is extra fun by combining crispy sweet potato cubes and steak cubes in bowls, and serving them with a tangy and creamy sauce for dipping.

8 oz (225 g) center-cut beef filet, cut into 2" (5-cm) cubes

Salt and freshly ground black pepper

1 tbsp (10 g) BBQ Rub and Seasoning with Coffee and Garlic

1 large sweet potato, cut into 1" (2.5-cm) cubes

2 tbsp (30 ml) olive oil, divided

1 white onion, sliced thinly

3 tbsp (12 g) chopped fresh parsley, for garnish

Magnifisauce, for serving

Preheat the oven to 450°F (230°C).

In a medium-sized bowl, combine the cubed steak with salt and pepper and the BBQ coffee rub. Set aside.

In another medium-sized bowl, combine the sweet potato, 1 tablespoon (15 ml) of the olive oil, and salt and pepper. Toss well, then arrange the sweet potato cubes in a single layer on a baking sheet. Roast for 15 minutes, toss, then continue to roast for 10 to 15 minutes, or until golden brown and crispy.

While the sweet potato roasts, heat the remaining tablespoon (15 ml) of olive oil in a large cast-iron skillet over medium heat.

Once the oil is shimmering, add the onion and sauté for 5 to 6 minutes. Then, add the cubed steak in a single layer and cook for 2 to 3 minutes per side, or until browned.

To serve, divide the roasted sweet potato and cooked steak between two bowls and garnish with fresh parsley. Serve with Magnifisauce for dipping.

SLOW COOKER THAI SWEET GINGER CHICKEN

PREP TIME: 5 minutes
COOK TIME: 3 hours
SERVINGS: 2

This is a tantalizingly tasty dish that's sure to satisfy any craving for bold, Asian-inspired flavors. Juicy, tender chicken breasts are slow-cooked in Trader Joe's Thai Sweet Ginger Sauce until they practically fall apart in your mouth. Served over fluffy jasmine rice or steamed vegetables, this comforting dish is a true crowd-pleaser.

2 boneless chicken breasts

1 (10.1-oz [299-ml]) bottle Thai Sweet Ginger Sauce

1 (10-oz [280-g]) package Frozen Jasmine Rice

2 tbsp (7 g) sliced green onion or (3 g) fresh chives, for garnish

In the bowl of a slow cooker, combine the chicken with the Thai sweet ginger sauce. Set the slow cooker to LOW for 3 hours.

When the chicken is about 5 minutes from being finished, cook the rice according to the package instructions.

To serve, divide the rice between two plates and place the chicken over the rice. Spoon some of the sauce from the slow cooker over the top and garnish with green onion.

NOTE: If you're looking for a veggie to serve this with, I love it with steamed cauliflower or broccoli. Snap peas are delicious with it too!

BOUJIE TOASTS

Elevate your toast game with these recipes that will make you feel as if you're dining at a fancy brunch spot in LA. I've taken the humble slice of bread and transformed it into a canvas for some seriously delicious and Instagram-worthy creations. From savory to sweet, I've got you covered with such recipes as Caramelized Onion Toast (page 44) and Charcuterie Toast (page 51).

These toasts are really popular on my Instagram and TikTok, and it is no wonder! They are visually stunning, full of vibrant flavors and easy to make. This is my favorite chapter of the whole book. I especially love the Mozzarella Medley Prosciutto Toast (page 43) and Roasted Cauliflower Toast (page 47), which are so different yet equally interesting and full-flavored.

So, put on your fancy pants and get ready to indulge in some seriously boujie toasts!

MOZZARELLA MEDLEY PROSCIUTTO TOAST

PREP TIME: 10 minutes

COOK TIME: 11 to 14 minutes

SERVINGS: 4

Indulge in the delicious combination of salty prosciutto and creamy marinated mozzarella with this "Red, White and Prosciutto" toast recipe. The cheese becomes oozing and melted in the oven while the prosciutto just warms through, resulting in a combination of smoky, salty and cheesy goodness that is great as part of a main meal or even for a tasty snack.

1 baguette, sliced into 2 (6" [15-cm]-long) pieces and then in half lengthwise

Olive oil, for cooking

3 tbsp (45 ml) Red Pepper Spread

12 oz (340 g) Marinated Fresh Mozzarella Cheese, sliced in half

4 thin slices prosciutto

Chopped fresh basil, for garnish

Preheat the oven to 400°F (200°C).

Brush a thin layer of olive oil over each slice of baguette and place them on a baking sheet. Toast in the oven for 3 to 4 minutes.

Remove the bread from the oven and spread a generous layer of Red Pepper Spread over each slice. Place the halved mozzarella balls, flat side down—you should be able to fit six to eight halves per baguette slice—over each piece of bread, return the bread to the oven and bake for 8 to 10 minutes, or until the cheese is melted.

About 2 minutes before removing the toasts from the oven, lay one slice of prosciutto over top of each slice of bread and continue to bake for about 2 minutes. When the prosciutto is warm, remove the toasts from the oven and garnish with basil.

NOTE: Use any leftover baguette for other toast recipes or to serve with pasta.

CARAMELIZED ONION TOAST

PREP TIME: 5 minutes
COOK TIME: 25 to 30 minutes
SERVINGS: 4

Sweet and sticky caramelized onions, delicious cheese studded with more onions, plus creamy onion dip. Just slap it all on slices of crusty baguette and you will have cheesy toasts reminiscent of heartwarming French onion soup. A little fresh thyme adds color and cuts through the richness of the toasts, but you can feel free to garnish with another herb, such as parsley, if that's what you have on hand instead.

2 tbsp (28 g) unsalted butter

1 tbsp (15 ml) extra virgin olive oil, plus more for cooking

2 large yellow onions, sliced very thinly

½ tsp kosher salt

1 baguette, sliced into 2 (6" [15-cm]-long) pieces and then in half lengthwise

3 tbsp (45 g) Caramelized Onion Dip

2 cups (225 g) shredded Cheddar Cheese with Caramelized Onions

¼ tsp red pepper flakes, for garnish

Fresh thyme, for garnish

In a large nonstick skillet, heat the butter and olive oil over medium heat. Add the onions and salt, and sauté, tossing occasionally, for 5 minutes, or until they begin to soften.

Allow the onions to cook for 20 to 25 minutes, tossing about every 5 minutes, until caramelized.

When the onions reach about the 12-minute point, preheat the oven to 375°F (190°C) and brush a thin layer of olive oil on both sides of the sliced baguette. Spread a thin layer of the Caramelized Onion Dip over each slice of baguette, top with the shredded cheese and toast directly on the middle rack in the oven for 6 to 10 minutes, or until the bread is toasted to your liking.

Divide the caramelized onions equally among the pieces of toasted baguette and garnish with red pepper flakes and thyme.

NOTES

- I used a mandoline to slice my onions, so they are paper-thin and caramelize quickly. If your onions are sliced thicker, they may take longer to caramelize.

- You can cook the onions ahead of time and store them in an airtight container in the refrigerator for 3 to 4 days.

- Sometimes, I like to add fresh greens or a fried egg.

- Turn this into a caramelized onion pizza, using Trader Joe's Plain Pizza Dough.

ROASTED CAULIFLOWER TOAST

PREP TIME: 10 minutes
COOK TIME: 30 to 38 minutes
SERVINGS: 6

For a tasty, cheesy snack or lunch, try these roasted cauliflower toasts, which have a dusting of chili-rich Ajika Georgian Seasoning Blend and paprika, plus oozing mascarpone and Gruyère cheese. These toasts are wonderful alongside a steaming bowl of soup, such as roasted tomato with basil, and are the most wondrous vegetarian meal.

4 cups (400 g) cauliflower florets, no bigger than 1" (2.5-cm) pieces

3 tbsp (45 ml) extra virgin olive oil, plus more for cooking

2 tbsp (12 g) Ajika Georgian Seasoning Blend

1½ tsp (9 g) kosher salt, divided

1 tsp freshly ground black pepper, divided

8 oz (225 g) mascarpone cheese, at room temperature

1 cup (120 g) shredded Gruyère cheese

6 slices of sourdough bread

1½ tsp (4 g) paprika

¼ cup (25 g) grated Parmesan cheese

3 tbsp minced (9 g) fresh chives

Coarse sea salt

Preheat the oven to 400°F (200°C). On a baking sheet, toss the cauliflower florets with olive oil, the Ajika seasoning, ½ teaspoon of kosher salt and ½ teaspoon of pepper. Spread out the cauliflower into a single layer and roast for 25 to 30 minutes, tossing once at about the 15-minute point, until the florets are tender and starting to brown.

When done, transfer the roasted cauliflower to a large bowl and add the mascarpone, stirring to coat the florets evenly. Then, mix in the shredded Gruyère, the remaining teaspoon (6 g) of kosher salt and the remaining ½ teaspoon of pepper. Set the mixture aside while you toast the bread.

Brush each slice of bread with a thin layer of olive oil and toast the bread on the top rack of the oven for 3 to 4 minutes, or until lightly browned. Transfer the toasted bread, in a single layer, to a foil-lined baking sheet.

Set the oven to BROIL and move the rack about 4 inches (10 cm) below the heating element.

Divide the cauliflower mixture equally among the pieces of toast and sprinkle with the paprika. Broil the cauliflower toasts for 2 to 4 minutes, until browned and bubbling. Keep a close eye on them!

To serve, transfer the cauliflower toast to a serving plate and sprinkle with the Parmesan cheese, chives and coarse sea salt. Serve hot.

NOTE: You can make the cauliflower mixture ahead of time and keep it in the refrigerator for 1 to 2 days.

CHILI CRUNCH FRIED EGGS ON TOAST

PREP TIME: 5 minutes
COOK TIME: 7 to 11 minutes
SERVINGS: 2

Just imagine breaking egg yolks and having them ooze over your bread, mixing with kimchi and other toppings, for savory, saucy, briny spiciness in every bite. These tasty toasts are perfect for those who love the bold flavors of kimchi, miso, garlic butter and chili along with their eggs. The Garlic Spread & Dip caramelizes on the bread while they are toasting for a sweet and smoky flavor.

2 tbsp (28 g) Garlic Spread & Dip

2 slices sourdough bread

2 tbsp (28 g) unsalted butter

1 tbsp (16 g) miso paste

2 tbsp (36 g) Crunchy Chili Onion

¼ cup (63 g) kimchi

2 large eggs

2 tbsp (7 g) sliced green onion

Preheat the oven to 400°F (200°C). Evenly spread the Garlic Spread & Dip over the bread and toast directly on the middle rack for 3 to 5 minutes, or until it's toasted to your liking. Alternatively, you can do this in an air fryer at 375°F (190°C).

Meanwhile, heat a nonstick skillet over medium heat, then add the butter and miso paste. Stir until the butter is melted and combined with the miso paste.

Stir in the Crunchy Chili Onion, then the kimchi. Crack both eggs into the pan over the kimchi. Cover and cook for 1 to 2 minutes to help the white part solidify, then continue to cook, uncovered, for 3 to 4 minutes, or until cooked to your liking.

Divide the kimchi and fried eggs between both pieces of toasted bread. Then, top with green onion and serve.

NOTES

- I like to add an extra egg and break the yolk in one of the eggs because I think it creates the perfect egg–to–runny yolk ratio.

- If you have Trader Joe's Black Garlic Seasoning, add some of that on top, too!

- If you want to cut down on the sodium, you can omit the Garlic Spread & Dip or sub 1½ tsp (8 g) salt for the miso paste.

CHARCUTERIE TOAST

PREP TIME: 5 minutes
COOK TIME: 7 to 9 minutes
SERVINGS: 2

Craving charcuterie but can't eat an entire board by yourself? This boujie charcuterie toast will satisfy all your cheesy cravings! With a crusty baguette base, creamy herb and cheese spread, piled high with your favorite meat and cheese, this toast is perfect for a solo snack or a fancy appetizer at your next party. Plus, it's super easy to customize with your favorite charcuterie items, so you can create a different masterpiece every time.

2 slices sourdough bread

2 tbsp (40 g) Hot & Sweet Pepper Jelly

5 to 6 oz (140 to 170 g) Goat Milk Brie Cheese, sliced thinly, OR creamy blue cheese

4 thin slices prosciutto

2 tbsp (14 g) finely chopped Marcona almonds

½ tsp minced fresh rosemary

Preheat the oven to 350°F (180°C).

On a baking sheet, arrange the bread in a single layer and toast for 3 to 4 minutes.

Once toasted to your liking, remove the bread from the oven and spread a tablespoon (20 g) of pepper jelly on each slice. Spread the cheese on top and bake for 4 to 5 minutes, or until the cheese is melted and bubbly.

Top with the prosciutto, chopped Marcona almonds and rosemary.

NOTES

- If you're a pickle lover, slice up a cornichon (charcuterie pickle) and nestle it under the prosciutto, for an oddly satisfying bite.

- Give this toast a try with any of your favorite charcuterie meats.

SMASHED PEA TOAST

PREP TIME: 10 minutes
COOK TIME: 7 to 9 minutes
SERVINGS: 2

Vibrant peas with rich herbs and garlic on toast is the perfect way to add a little green to your snack routine. Sourdough bread serves as the crunchy base. This recipe is great when you want something light, but satisfying—perfect for when you're feeling snacky but can't quite put your finger on what you're craving. Plus, it's a fun and unique way to enjoy nutritious peas that'll have you feeling like a kid again (but with way better taste buds). Top it all off with feta, a squeeze of lemon juice and some chopped parsley and chives, and you've got yourself a picture-perfect snack that's as delicious as it is adorable.

2 slices sourdough bread

¾ cup (98 g) frozen peas

1 clove garlic, chopped

½ cup (120 ml) water

¼ tsp kosher salt

2 tbsp (8 g) chopped fresh parsley, plus more for garnish

2 tbsp (6 g) chopped fresh chives, plus more for garnish

¼ cup (60 ml) olive oil, plus more for drizzling

¼ cup (38 g) crumbled feta cheese

¼ tsp red pepper flakes

Juice of ½ lemon

Toast the bread for 4 to 5 minutes, or until toasted to your liking.

In a small saucepan, combine the peas, garlic and water. Cook over medium heat, stirring occasionally, until the peas are tender, 3 to 4 minutes. Drain the peas and garlic, transfer to a food processor and add the salt, parsley, chives and olive oil. Pulse until a coarse paste forms, scraping down the sides as needed.

Divide the smashed peas equally between each slice of toast and top with the feta cheese, a drizzle of oil, the red pepper flakes, a squeeze of lemon juice and more parsley and chives.

NOTES

- The pea mash can be made a day ahead of time and stored in an airtight container in the refrigerator.
- You can also use other fresh herbs, such as dill or mint.
- Garlic Spread & Dip tastes delicious under the smashed peas!

PERFECTLY DRESSED RAVIOLI

Dress up your ravioli with these quick and easy sauces! Whether you're cooking for a busy weeknight or hosting a dinner party, these recipes are sure to impress. After all, everything *is* better with sauce. Using Trader Joe's delicious and convenient ravioli as a base, these sauces are the perfect finishing touch. From classic Brown Butter Sage Sauce (page 57) to Pesto Perfecto Sauce (page 65), you'll find a sauce for every mood and occasion. Whip up a batch of one of these sauces in minutes, and you'll have a flavorful and satisfying meal on your plate in no time.

I get asked a lot about which sauces are best to pair with the Trader Joe's ravioli, and while there's no one size fits all, the sauces in this chapter will work for most of their delicious selections! These sauces are simple to put together and make the ravioli a little less like boxed ravioli and more like restaurant ravioli. They would all work with other types of pasta, too, though, so let your imagination and creativity run wild!

BROWN BUTTER SAGE SAUCE

PREP TIME: 5 minutes
COOK TIME: 10 minutes
SERVINGS: 2

There's almost nothing this doesn't pair well with, so it's perfect for dressing up Trader Joe's ravioli! The rich, nutty flavor of browned butter goes perfectly with the earthy aroma of fresh sage, creating a velvety smooth sauce. It's kind of like herb-flavored butter, except it becomes a flavorful, bubbling mixture for cooked ravioli to bathe in. The Butternut Squash Ravioli is my favorite to pair this sauce with! It's equally tasty drizzled over grilled steak or roasted pork chops as well.

½ cup (114 g) salted butter

1 small clove garlic, minced

4 to 5 fresh sage leaves, stemmed and julienned

Freshly ground black pepper

Cooked ravioli of your choice, for serving

In a medium-sized skillet, heat the butter over medium heat. Once the butter is melted, add the garlic and sage, plus pepper to taste, giving it a quick stir with a wooden spoon.

Let the butter cook until it begins to brown, but be careful not to overcook. A light golden-brown color is perfect.

Remove the sauce from the heat and add the cooked ravioli to the pan, tossing to coat.

Divide the ravioli between two plates and serve.

PAIRING SUGGESTIONS: This sauce works well with most Trader Joe's Fall ravioli. My favorites to pair it with are the Butternut Squash Ravioli, Cacio e Pepe Ravioli, Ricotta & Spinach Filled Ravioli and Mushroom Ravioli with Mushroom Truffle Sauce.

LIQUID GARLIC BUTTER GOLD

PREP TIME: 5 minutes
COOK TIME: 10 minutes
SERVINGS: 2

Packed with rich, buttery goodness and a punch of garlicky flavor, this sauce is perfect for just about any ravioli, as well as for any dish, from pasta to seafood, and will leave you feeling satisfied and happy. If you want to keep extra sauce on hand for later, you can freeze it in an ice cube tray.

½ cup (114 g) unsalted butter

2 Frozen Garlic Cubes

½ cup white cooking wine

1½ tbsp (6 g) chopped fresh parsley

1 tsp salt

1 tsp freshly ground black pepper

Cooked ravioli of your choice, for serving

In a medium-sized saucepan, melt the butter over medium heat. Then, stir in the garlic cubes, white wine, parsley, salt and pepper.

Remove the saucepan from the heat and serve warm, or let cool and then divide into an ice cube tray and store in the freezer.

PAIRING SUGGESTIONS: Lobster Ravioli, Mushroom Ravioli with Mushroom Truffle Sauce, Ricotta & Lemon Zest Ravioli and Sweet Corn, Burrata & Basil Ravioli.

GORGONZOLA CREAM SAUCE

PREP TIME: 5 minutes
COOK TIME: 10 to 12 minutes
SERVINGS: 2

The earthiness of salty, pungent Gorgonzola cheese is rounded out with white wine, cream, nutmeg and parsley for a sauce that works with many different types of pasta, but is particularly good with Trader Joe's 4 Cheese Ravioli. I really love sautéing some mushrooms to go with it, too. The sauce is tangy, rich and creamy, and oh so delicious! Even those who aren't usually drawn to blue-veined stinky cheeses will likely appreciate the complexity of this simple yet decadent sauce.

1 tbsp (15 ml) olive oil

1 large shallot, diced

1 tbsp (15 ml) white cooking wine

1 cup (240 ml) heavy cream

6 oz (170 g) Gorgonzola cheese, crumbled

¼ tsp ground nutmeg

3 tbsp (12 g) minced flat-leaf parsley

Salt and freshly ground black pepper

Cooked ravioli of your choice, for serving

In a large skillet, heat the olive oil over medium heat. Add the shallot and sauté until soft, 4 to 5 minutes, then add the cooking wine and continue to sauté for 30 to 45 seconds before adding the cream, Gorgonzola cheese and nutmeg. Bring the sauce to a simmer, stirring frequently, to help melt the cheese. Simmer for 5 to 7 minutes, or until the cheese is completely melted.

Remove the pan from the heat and mix in the parsley, salt and pepper to taste, then the cooked ravioli. Toss to coat the ravioli and divide between two plates.

NOTE: A squeeze of lemon juice is really nice in this sauce and can add a bright and acidic element to balance out the richness of the cheese and cream.

PAIRING SUGGESTIONS: Pumpkin Ravioli, Mushroom Ravioli with Mushroom Truffle Sauce or Ricotta & Lemon Zest Ravioli.

CREAM OF 'SHROOM SAUCE

PREP TIME: 2 minutes
COOK TIME: 12 to 14 minutes
SERVINGS: 2

I love mushrooms so much, so this sauce is truly one of my favorites. It has garlic, mushrooms and heavy cream to make it the most luxe sauce ever. Despite the cream, it's still a rather brothy sauce that doesn't feel too heavy. So, what's not to love about this meatless combination that has a meaty texture and well-rounded flavor? The golden mushrooms are absolutely heavenly with any cheese ravioli—pure comfort in a bowl!

2 tbsp (28 g) unsalted butter

2 Frozen Garlic Cubes

12 oz (340 g) cremini mushrooms, sliced thinly

1 tbsp (15 ml) white cooking wine

1 cup (240 ml) vegetable broth

½ cup (120 ml) heavy cream

Salt and freshly ground black pepper

Cooked ravioli of your choice

Fresh parsley, for garnish

In a large saucepan, heat the butter and garlic over medium heat until the butter has melted.

Add the mushrooms and sauté for 8 to 10 minutes, or until browned. Then, add the white cooking wine and toss the mushrooms for 30 seconds.

Pour in the vegetable broth and cream. Mix to combine and season to taste with salt and pepper. Simmer for 2 minutes, then add the cooked ravioli and toss to coat.

Divide the ravioli between two plates and garnish with parsley.

PAIRING SUGGESTIONS: Mushroom Ravioli with Mushroom Truffle Sauce, Roasted Cauliflower & Cheese Ravioli or Ricotta & Lemon Zest Ravioli.

PESTO PERFECTO SAUCE

PREP TIME: 2 minutes
COOK TIME: 8 to 11 minutes
SERVINGS: 2

For a tomato-y sauce that is ready in a flash, try this creamy tomato pesto sauce. It uses Trader Joe's Pesto Rosso, which is tangy, vibrant and delicious on its own but is elevated with the additions of caramelized shallot and heavy cream for some sweet savoriness and richness.

1 tbsp (15 ml) olive oil

1 shallot, sliced thinly

½ cup (106 g) Pesto Rosso

¼ cup (60 ml) heavy cream

½ cup (120 ml) vegetable broth

Salt and freshly ground black pepper

Cooked ravioli of your choice

2 tbsp (6 g) chopped fresh basil

In a medium-sized skillet, heat the olive oil over medium heat. When hot, add the shallot and sauté, tossing occasionally, for 4 to 6 minutes, or until it begins to caramelize.

Lower the heat to medium-low and add the pesto, cream and vegetable broth to the pan. Stir to combine and heat, stirring occasionally, for 3 to 4 minutes, or until the sauce is heated through.

Season with salt and pepper to taste, then add the cooked ravioli of your choice and toss to coat.

Divide the ravioli between two plates and garnish with basil.

NOTE: Add a tablespoon (9 g) of Calabrian chile pepper or a pinch of red pepper flakes to provide a little kick to your sauce.

PAIRING SUGGESTIONS: 4 Cheese Ravioli, Spinach Tortellini, Sweet Corn, Burrata & Basil Ravioli or Cacio e Pepe Ravioli.

EVENING MUNCHIES

Get ready to satisfy those snack cravings! These small bites are perfect for sharing with friends or enjoying as a solo snack attack. Using the tastiest Trader Joe's ingredients, these recipes will take your taste buds on a wild ride.

Several of these recipes only take minutes to prepare, such as the Everything Bagel Cucumber Bites (page 70) and the Charcoochie Sticks (page 77), which are basically the components of charcuterie on toothpicks for a tasty party bite (these are so good!). They make wonderful quick snacks or last-minute hors d'oeuvres that will wow your guests and make your home the place people will stop in unexpectedly, hoping for more craveable bites of deliciousness.

PEACH AND BURRATA FLATBREAD

PREP TIME: 15 minutes
COOK TIME: 16 to 21 minutes
SERVINGS: 2

Burrata is my favorite cheese ever! It is literally life to me, so I obviously had to give it main character energy in my book. Here, we have a crispy crust slathered in Trader Joe's Garlic Spread & Dip that caramelizes in the oven, topped with salty prosciutto, peppery arugula and luscious slices of juicy peaches. You won't be able to resist taking a big bite. And the pièce de résistance? A generous dollop of creamy burrata cheese, sprinkled with freshly ground black pepper and drizzled with tangy balsamic glaze. This flatbread is so good, it'll make you want to peach for the stars!

4 thin slices prosciutto

1 Pizza Crust

3 tbsp (42 g) Garlic Spread & Dip

1½ cups (30 g) baby arugula

Juice of ½ lemon

2 tbsp (30 ml) extra virgin olive oil

¼ tsp kosher salt

1 fresh peach, thinly sliced

4 oz (115 g) burrata cheese

Freshly ground black pepper

Balsamic glaze, for drizzling

Preheat the oven to 400°F (200°C) and line a baking sheet with foil.

On the prepared baking sheet, arrange the prosciutto in a single layer and bake for 12 to 15 minutes, flipping at about the 7-minute point, until crispy.

When 6 minutes remain for the prosciutto, evenly spread the Garlic Spread & Dip over the pizza crust and place directly on the oven rack, next to the prosciutto, for 4 to 6 minutes, or until lightly toasted. Use tongs to remove the crust from the oven and carefully transfer it to a separate baking sheet. Remove the prosciutto from the oven when crispy and let cool for a few minutes before chopping, leaving the oven on.

Meanwhile, in a medium-sized bowl, toss together the baby arugula, lemon juice, olive oil and salt until well combined.

To assemble, layer the arugula and sliced peaches over the pizza crust and bake for 3 to 4 minutes.

Sprinkle the chopped prosciutto over the peaches and arugula, then tear the burrata into small pieces and arrange over top. Top with pepper to taste and a drizzle of balsamic glaze.

NOTES

- If you're making this recipe when peaches aren't in season, you can use Trader Joe's Peach Halves. They're in a jar in the dry goods section of the store! You can also use frozen peaches (thawed first) if you like

- I love using Trader Joe's Truffle Burrata in this recipe when it's in season.

EVERYTHING BAGEL CUCUMBER BITES

PREP TIME: 15 minutes
COOK TIME: 0 minutes
SERVINGS: 20

If you're an Everything but the Bagel lover, you will adore these unique cucumber bites topped with cream cheese, Trader Joe's Everything but the Bagel Seasoned Smoked Salmon and fresh herbs. The crunchy cucumber slices are refreshing and texturally interesting against the soft smoked salmon and smooth cream cheese. Try making a batch for your next party and switch up the garnishes by adding some avocado, capers or crumbled feta cheese.

1 large cucumber

1 (4-oz [113-g]) package Everything but the Bagel Seasoned Smoked Salmon, sliced into 1" (2.5-cm) pieces

½ cup (100 g) whipped cream cheese

¼ cup (12 g) diced fresh chives or (16 g) fresh dill

Slice the cucumber into 1-inch (2.5-cm)-thick rounds.

Top the cucumber slices with a piece of smoked salmon, a dollop of cream cheese and chives.

NOTE: Depending on the size of your cucumber and how thickly you cut it, you may not have exactly 20 slices. Just make as many bites as you can with the slices you have!

GREEK MEATBALL SKEWERS

PREP TIME: 15 minutes
COOK TIME: 15 to 20 minutes
SERVINGS: 10 skewers

Get ready to travel to the Mediterranean with these flavor-packed Greek meatball skewers loaded with colorful veggies and creamy tzatziki. And forget the grill—this recipe takes a new twist with each component cooked separately in a sizzling pan, allowing you to create a delicious, easy-to-make appetizer that will make you feel like a Greek god or goddess in the kitchen!

2 tbsp (30 ml) olive oil, divided

Salt and freshly ground black pepper

2 green bell peppers, seeded and cut into 1" (2.5-cm) squares

2 red bell peppers, seeded and cut into 1" (2.5-cm) squares

2 red onions, cut into 1" (2.5-cm) squares

1 (20-oz [567-g]) package Frozen Party Size Mini Meatballs

Tzatziki, for drizzling

3 tbsp (12 g) minced fresh dill

Preheat the oven to 375°F (190°C). Meanwhile, in a large bowl, combine 1 tablespoon (15 ml) of the olive oil with the salt and black pepper, sliced bell peppers and onions.

On a rimmed baking sheet, arrange the seasoned peppers and onions in a single layer and bake for 15 to 20 minutes, or until tender and beginning to brown.

Meanwhile, in a large, heavy-bottomed skillet, heat the remaining tablespoon (15 ml) of olive oil over medium heat.

Place the meatballs in the skillet, tossing to coat with the oil. Cover with a tight-fitting lid and cook for 6 minutes. Remove the lid and continue to cook the meatballs, tossing occasionally, for 8 to 10 minutes, or until fully heated through.

Once the vegetables and meatballs are cooked, thread them onto the wooden skewers, alternating between meatballs and vegetables.

Drizzle the tzatziki onto the skewers and garnish with dill.

KALE PESTO BURRATA FLATBREAD

PREP TIME: 5 minutes
COOK TIME: 8 to 11 minutes
SERVINGS: 2

Homemade pizza is a breeze when you have Trader Joe's Pizza Crust and Vegan Kale, Cashew & Basil Pesto for the base, and top it with a mixture of fresh arugula, tomato and burrata. The pepperiness of the arugula pairs beautifully with the salty, creamy burrata and earthy pesto. Some of the ingredients for this recipe overlap with those of the Peach and Burrata Flatbread (page 69), so you can plan to make that one the next day!

1½ tbsp (23 ml) extra virgin olive oil, plus more for brushing and cooking

1 Pizza Crust

½ cup (120 g) Vegan Kale, Cashew & Basil Pesto

1 tomato, sliced thinly

¾ tsp kosher salt, divided

1½ cups (30 g) baby arugula

Juice of ½ lemon

1 ball burrata cheese

Preheat the oven to 425°F (220°C). Lightly brush the top of the pizza crust with a thin layer of olive oil. Evenly spread the pesto over the pizza crust and bake directly on the oven rack for 5 to 6 minutes, or until lightly toasted.

Meanwhile, sprinkle the tomato slices with ½ teaspoon of the salt. In a medium-sized bowl, toss the baby arugula with the olive oil, the remaining ¼ teaspoon of salt and the lemon juice.

Using tongs, carefully transfer the crust from the oven rack to a baking sheet. Then, arrange the arugula and sliced tomato on the pizza and bake on the pan for 3 to 5 more minutes, or until the crust is crisp.

Slice the pizza into strips, then tear the burrata and place it on top of the pizza.

CHARCOOCHIE STICKS

PREP TIME: 15 minutes
COOK TIME: 0 minutes
SERVINGS: 20

Presenting the charcuterie board on a stick (with a fun name), here to elevate your appetizer game! They're perfect for when you're craving a fancy spread, but don't want to deal with the hassle of a full charcuterie board. These sticks are loaded with all your favorite meats, cheeses and accoutrements, all stacked on a stick for easy snacking. Whether you just want to elevate your snacks or are hosting a party, these are a fun way to enhance your culinary experience and impress your guests!

1 lb (455 g) thinly sliced prosciutto

10 Mini Brie Bites, halved

12 oz (340 g) Fire Roasted Red Peppers, cut into 2" (5-cm) squares

12 oz (340 g) Marinated Fresh Mozzarella Cheese

20 cherry tomatoes

1 baguette, sliced into rounds

On 20 skewers, thread half a slice of prosciutto, followed by a halved Brie Bite, a red pepper square, a mozzarella ball, the remaining prosciutto, a cherry tomato and a slice of baguette.

NOTE: You can swap the cherry tomatoes with olives; just be sure to use pitted olives.

CRISPY AIR FRYER RAVIOLI

PREP TIME: 10 minutes
COOK TIME: 20 minutes
SERVINGS: 2

These golden ravioli have a crispy bread crumb coating flavored with nutty Parmesan cheese and fragrant Italian seasoning. Trader Joe's has a frozen version of fried ravioli that is deep fried before being frozen. My version is air fried, making it a healthier option. Served with a tangy marinara sauce, these are crispy packages of perfection, great for an appetizer with friends and are easy to scale up or down.

1 cup (115 g) dried bread crumbs

1 tsp Italian seasoning

2 large eggs

1 (10-oz [283-g]) package 4 Cheese Ravioli

Olive oil cooking spray

1 cup (245 g) marinara sauce

1 tbsp (4 g) chopped fresh parsley

2 tbsp (10 g) grated Parmesan cheese

Preheat an air fryer to 350°F (180°C). In a shallow bowl, mix the bread crumbs and Italian seasoning. Crack the eggs into another shallow bowl and beat lightly with a whisk or a fork. Dip the ravioli into the eggs, and then into the bread crumb mixture, patting with your hands to help the coating stick.

Working in batches, spray the tray in the air fryer basket with olive oil spray, then arrange the ravioli in a single layer and spritz them with olive oil. Air fry the ravioli for 3 minutes. Flip the ravioli, spritz with olive oil again and cook until golden brown, about 3 minutes longer.

Meanwhile, in a small saucepan, heat the marinara sauce over medium heat for 5 minutes, or until warm.

Transfer the ravioli to a serving plate and garnish with parsley and a sprinkle of Parmesan cheese. Serve with warm marinara sauce on the side.

NOTES

- Be careful of ravioli that may be stuck together. If they are stuck, carefully pull them apart, being mindful not to rip any open.

- If you prefer to fry the ravioli in oil, using a deep cast-iron skillet, heat ½ inch (1.3 cm) of oil to 375°F (190°C). Fry the ravioli, a few at a time, for 1 to 2 minutes per side, or until golden brown.

CRISPY STREET CORN SMASHED POTATOES

PREP TIME: 10 minutes
COOK TIME: 47 to 58 minutes
SERVINGS: 4

Loaded with fire-roasted corn, briny Cotija cheese and Sriracha mayonnaise, these potatoes make a fiesta in your mouth! With a hint of spice and a sprinkle of fresh herbs, they're the perfect way to add a touch of zing to any meal. Consider serving these loaded potatoes as a side dish or a fun snack.

1 lb (455 g) baby potatoes

3 tbsp (45 ml) olive oil, divided

½ tsp kosher salt, plus a pinch

2½ tbsp (24 g) Everything but the Elote Seasoning Blend, divided

1½ cups (195 g) Frozen Roasted Corn

1 tbsp (15 g) Sriracha

1 tbsp (15 g) mayonnaise

3 tbsp (23 g) crumbled Cotija cheese

3 tbsp (3 g) chopped fresh cilantro

Preheat the oven to 450°F (230°C).

Place the potatoes in a large pot and fill it with cold water. Bring the water to a boil over medium-high heat. Then, lower the heat to medium-low and simmer the potatoes until they are just barely fork-tender, 15 to 20 minutes. Drain the potatoes and let them cool slightly.

Brush two baking sheets with 1½ tablespoons (23 g) of the olive oil. Divide the potatoes between the two pans. Using the bottom of a glass, gently smash each potato once, trying to keep it in one piece. Drizzle 1 tablespoon (15 ml) of olive oil over the potatoes, then season them with the salt and about 2 tablespoons (19 g) of the Everything but the Elote Seasoning Blend.

Place the potatoes in the oven and roast for 30 to 35 minutes, or until golden and crispy.

While the potatoes roast, in a medium-sized skillet, heat the remaining 1½ teaspoons (7 ml) of the olive oil over medium-high heat. Add the corn to the pan and toss to coat in the olive oil. Season the corn with the remaining 1½ teaspoons (5 g) of Everything but the Elote Seasoning Blend and the pinch of salt, and cook, stirring occasionally, for 2 to 3 minutes.

When the potatoes are ready, remove them from the oven, transfer them to a serving plate and top them with the cooked corn. Combine the Sriracha and mayonnaise in a small bowl. Then drizzle the mixture over the potatoes. Finish with the crumbled Cotija cheese and cilantro.

LOADED WAFFLE FRIES

PREP TIME: 5 minutes
COOK TIME: 20 to 25 minutes
SERVINGS: 4

Similar to In-N-Out's Animal Style® Fries, these include the flavors of onion and cheese, plus a creamy sauce, loaded on top of crispy fries. But, they are even more fun made with waffle fries! I mean, who doesn't love potatoes in the form of lattices that are crispy on the outside and fluffy on the inside? These are wonderfully extravagant and perfect served on their own or alongside a juicy, home-cooked burger.

20 oz (567 g) Frozen Seasoned Waffle Cut Fries

2 tbsp (28 g) unsalted butter

1 large white onion, diced

3 to 4 slices American cheese

½ cup (128 g) Magnifisauce

1 to 2 tbsp (15 to 30 g) sweet relish

Preheat the oven to 400°F (200°C). On a baking sheet, arrange the waffle fries in a single layer. Bake for 20 to 25 minutes, or until crispy.

Meanwhile, in a nonstick skillet, melt the butter over medium heat. Then, add the onion and toss to coat with the butter. Cook, tossing occasionally, for 15 to 20 minutes, or until caramelized.

When the waffle fries are done, make a pile with them in the center of your baking sheet. I like to transfer mine to a cast-iron pan for this step.

Layer the American cheese slices evenly on top of the waffle fries. Broil on HIGH for 3 to 5 minutes, or until the cheese is melted.

Meanwhile, in a small bowl combine the Magnifisauce and relish, then set aside.

Remove the cheesy fries from the oven and top with the caramelized onion and Magnifisauce mixture. Serve them hot.

TURKEY APPLE CHEDDAR PINWHEELS

PREP TIME: 15 minutes
COOK TIME: 0 minutes
SERVINGS: 2

These pinwheels are the ultimate in portable snack luxury—layers of turkey, Cheddar cheese and crisp apple all rolled up in a cozy tortilla blanket, ready to accompany you on any adventure. It's like a flavor parade in your mouth, complete with a marching band of zesty spices and a confetti of crispy veggies. So, go ahead and take a bite—the party is just getting started!

4 oz (115 g) Unexpected Cheddar Cheese Spread

4 (12-inch [30-cm]) burrito tortillas

8 oz (225 g) thinly sliced deli turkey breast

8 oz (225 g) lettuce or mixed greens, any kind you like

1 Fuji apple, sliced very thinly

Evenly spread a generous layer of Unexpected Cheddar Cheese Spread over each tortilla (to the edges), then lay three or four slices of turkey breast flat on top of the Cheddar spread in a single layer. Arrange the lettuce and apple slices in the middle of each tortilla in a single layer.

Roll up the tortillas gently yet tightly to make sure they hold together and keep their shape.

Cut off the ends of each tortilla roll and cut the rolls into 1-inch (2.5-cm) slices.

NOTE: Try using a mandoline to slice the apple, to get perfectly thin slices that are flexible for rolling.

EVERYTHING BUT THE LEFTOVERS FRENCH FRY POUTINE

PREP TIME: 10 minutes
COOK TIME: 20 minutes
SERVINGS: 2

Indulge in the ultimate comfort food with this poutine! Crispy golden fries are smothered in rich gravy and topped with all your favorite Thanksgiving flavors—turkey, mushrooms, fresh herbs and Trader Joe's Everything but the Leftovers Seasoning Blend. It's everything you love about Thanksgiving dinner, but in one deliciously decadent package. So, grab a fork (or just dig in with your hands; I won't judge) and get ready to satisfy your taste buds with Thanksgiving flavors any time of year.

---

1 (24-oz [680-g]) bag frozen french fries

1 tbsp (15 ml) olive oil

10 oz (280 g) cremini mushrooms, diced

¼ tsp kosher salt

1 tbsp (15 ml) white cooking wine

11 oz (310 g) Condensed Cream of Portabella Mushroom Soup

½ cup (120 ml) vegetable broth

1½ tsp (7 g) Everything but the Leftovers Seasoning Blend

1 cup (175 g) shredded leftover turkey

Fresh herbs, such as parsley or thyme, for garnish

Cook the french fries according to the package instructions. I cooked mine almost double the time suggested on the package (about 25 minutes).

While the french fries bake, make your mushroom gravy: In a medium-sized skillet, heat the olive oil over medium-high heat. Add the mushrooms and salt, and sauté for 7 to 10 minutes, or until the mushrooms brown. Deglaze the pan with the cooking wine, scraping the browned bits off the bottom.

In the skillet, heat the cream of mushroom soup, stirring frequently, for 2 to 3 minutes, or until heated through. Lower the heat to medium and stir in the vegetable broth. The mixture should have a thick, gravylike consistency.

When the french fries are ready, toss them with the Everything but the Leftovers Seasoning Blend before transferring them to a large serving dish. Add your shredded turkey on top. Pour the mushroom gravy over the turkey and french fries and garnish with your fresh herbs before serving.

NOTES

- If your gravy is ready before the french fries, keep it on the lowest heat setting and stir occasionally to keep it from getting too thick.

- The frozen french fries overcrowded my largest baking sheet; I recommend using two pans, so they crisp instead of steam and get soggy.

- If your gravy is too thick, add more vegetable broth until it reaches your desired consistency.

BRUSSELS SPROUTS FLATBREAD

PREP TIME: 10 minutes
COOK TIME: 10 to 13 minutes
SERVINGS: 2

Brussels sprouts, which many choose to either love or hate, gets the all-star treatment with plenty of bacon, melty cheese and tangy balsamic drizzle, all assembled as a flatbread pizza. The added bacon and cheese really do change the game, elevating the humble sprout to something worthy of a gastropub. And don't skimp on the balsamic glaze. The combo of sweet, tangy, salty and smoky is something else!

¼ cup (56 g) Garlic Spread & Dip

1 Pizza Crust

1 cup (88 g) shredded Brussels sprouts

1 tbsp (15 ml) extra virgin olive oil

5 cherry tomatoes, halved

2 strips thick-cut bacon, cooked and diced

½ cup (60 g) shredded Gruyère cheese

Balsamic glaze, for drizzling

Preheat the oven to 375°F (190°C). Evenly spread the Garlic Spread & Dip over the crust and bake for 6 to 8 minutes, or until the crust begins to toast.

In a medium-sized bowl, toss the shredded Brussels sprouts with the olive oil.

Remove the crust from the oven and top with the Brussels sprouts, cherry tomatoes, bacon and shredded cheese. Bake for 4 to 5 minutes, or until the cheese has melted and the crust is toasted to your liking.

Allow the flatbread to cool for about 2 minutes before slicing and drizzling with balsamic glaze.

NOTE: If you want to swap out the tomatoes for something else, try pickled onions or fresh sliced peaches for a unique twist.

BEYOND GREENS

The humble side dish is often overlooked, but can be as varied as the rainbow, involving anything from veggies and fruit to meat and cheese, and everything in between. Side dishes are wondrous in how they can round out a meal, whether they are salads full of crisp, raw vegetables or soft greens, or are a hot dish of cooked green beans adorned with garnishes like Cheddar cheese. This chapter includes a little of everything from a Roasted Red Pepper Pasta Salad (page 97) that contains Marinated Fresh Mozzarella Cheese balls, which just make your mouth water, to French Onion Slow Cooker Mashed Potatoes (page 101).

Some of the salads involve vegetable preparation that you might not be used to in a salad, such as roasting the broccoli in the Roasted Broccoli Salad (page 94), which is tossed with quinoa, raisins, feta cheese and more. The roasting process sweetens the broccoli so that it stands out more against all of the other components. Meanwhile, the Lemon Honey Carrot Ribbons salad (page 93) includes carrot ribbons reminiscent of noodles but with a vibrancy of color. I love how salads and side dishes can be interesting and varied, and add a lot of interest to a plate with roasted or grilled meat or seafood.

LEMON HONEY CARROT RIBBONS

PREP TIME: 10 minutes
COOK TIME: 0 minutes
SERVINGS: 4

When I polled my Instagram audience on what they'd like to see in this book, many of them requested salads without lettuce. So, I'm here to deliver! This one consists of carrots that are sliced into ribbons before being tossed with toasty sunflower seeds, green onions, feta cheese and a lemon honey dressing. This salad truly looks like sunshine on a plate! For the prettiest appearance, choose an array of rainbow carrots, such as purple, orange, red and yellow.

LEMON HONEY DRESSING

Juice of 1 lemon

¼ tsp kosher salt

½ tsp freshly ground black pepper

1 tbsp (15 ml) honey

2 tbsp (30 ml) extra virgin olive oil

SALAD

10 to 12 medium-sized carrots, sliced into ribbons

¼ cup (14 g) thinly sliced green onions

1 cup (145 g) roasted sunflower seeds

½ cup (75 g) crumbled feta cheese

Make the dressing: In a small bowl, whisk together the lemon juice, salt, pepper, honey and olive oil until smooth.

Make the salad: In a large bowl, combine the carrot ribbons, green onions and roasted sunflower seeds. Pour the dressing over the top and mix to combine. Then, gently mix in the crumbled feta before serving.

NOTE: Using a vegetable peeler or mandoline is the best way to make the carrot ribbons.

ROASTED BROCCOLI SALAD

PREP TIME: 5 minutes
COOK TIME: 15 minutes
SERVINGS: 4

Trust me, the act of roasting broccoli (or any other brassica, for that matter) deepens its flavor and gives it a meatier quality. Including crispy quinoa, fresh parsley, briny feta, golden raisins and a red wine vinaigrette, this salad is as wonderful on its own as it is paired with some seared steak or poached chicken or fish. Honestly, though, I could eat it on its own, no additions necessary.

2 cups (150 g) very finely chopped broccoli florets

2 tbsp (30 ml) extra virgin olive oil, divided

¼ cup (15 g) chopped fresh parsley, divided

½ tsp kosher salt

½ tsp freshly ground black pepper

¾ cup (139 g) cooked quinoa

4 oz (115 g) feta cheese, crumbled

½ cup (75 g) golden raisins

DRESSING

1 tbsp (15 ml) red wine vinegar

2 tbsp (30 ml) extra virgin olive oil

1 tbsp (15 ml) fresh lemon juice

1 clove garlic, minced

⅛ tsp ground cumin

⅛ tsp salt

Preheat the oven to 425°F (220°C).

On a rimmed baking sheet lined with foil, toss the broccoli, 1 tablespoon (15 ml) of the olive oil, half of the parsley, salt and pepper. On another rimmed baking sheet, toss the quinoa with the remaining tablespoon (15 ml) of the olive oil and arrange it in a flat layer. You can add a pinch of salt to the quinoa if you like, too.

Place both baking sheets in the oven and roast for 15 minutes, or until the broccoli begins to brown and the quinoa is brown and crispy.

Meanwhile, prepare the dressing: In a small bowl, combine the red wine vinegar, olive oil, lemon juice, garlic, cumin and salt.

Remove the broccoli and quinoa from the oven and let cool before transferring to a large serving bowl and mixing with as much dressing as you like, plus the feta cheese, raisins and remaining parsley.

NOTES

- This salad can be made a day in advance, but it tastes best when made fresh. The quinoa will not stay crispy after storing.

- You can swap out the broccoli for cauliflower, if you like.

ROASTED RED PEPPER PASTA SALAD

PREP TIME: 2 minutes
COOK TIME: 12 to 15 minutes
SERVINGS: 4

This Italian pasta salad is briny, fresh, herbaceous and cheesy with crispy prosciutto, capers, roasted red peppers, pesto and mozzarella. It's a wowing showstopper of a dish that is so delicious, it almost seems a crime that it takes very little effort at all (I'm not complaining). This is a great salad to use up whatever pasta you have in your pantry.

5 oz (140 g) thinly sliced prosciutto

1 lb (455 g) uncooked Fusilli Corti Bucati Pasta, or any short pasta of your choice

8 oz (225 g) Vegan Kale, Cashew & Basil Pesto

1 lb (455 g) jarred fire-roasted red peppers, drained and diced

8 oz (225 g) Marinated Mozzarella Balls, halved

¼ cup (34 g) drained capers

½ tsp red pepper flakes

¼ tsp kosher salt

½ tsp freshly ground black pepper

Preheat the oven to 400°F (200°C) and line a baking sheet with foil. Place the prosciutto in a single layer on the prepared baking sheet and bake, for 12 to 15 minutes, turning at about the 7-minute point, or until crispy. It's okay if the prosciutto isn't completely flat; it will still get crispy. When the prosciutto has finished cooking, remove from the oven and allow it to cool for about 5 minutes before dicing it.

While the prosciutto bakes, cook the pasta according to the package instructions. When cooked, reserve ¼ cup (60 ml) of the pasta water, then drain the pasta and rinse with cool water.

In a large serving bowl, combine the cooked pasta, pesto and reserved pasta water until the noodles are fully coated.

Add the red peppers, mozzarella balls, capers, red pepper flakes, salt and black pepper to the bowl, and toss to combine.

NOTES

- If you like your pasta salad super creamy, you can combine the pesto with ¼ cup (60 g) of mayonnaise, Greek yogurt or sour cream before mixing it in with the pasta.

- This pasta salad can be made ahead of time and kept in the refrigerator for 3 to 4 days. I recommend removing it from the fridge about an hour before serving.

5-MINUTE GARLICKY GREEN BEANS

PREP TIME: 2 minutes
COOK TIME: 2 to 3 minutes
SERVINGS: 4

All seekers of tasty green bean recipes, raise your hand! These green beans are extraordinarily simple and extraordinarily delicious with an abundance of Garlic Spread & Dip and Cheddar cheese. Even the pickiest eaters will adore their savory garlickiness. Keep this recipe close by when you're in need of a tasty side dish for anything from weeknight dinners to holiday gatherings!

1½ lb (680 g) fresh green beans

½ cup (112 g) Garlic Spread & Dip

Juice of ½ lemon

¼ cup (30 g) shredded Unexpected Cheddar Cheese

Bring a large pot of water to a boil over medium-high heat.

Add the green beans to the boiling water and cook for 2 to 3 minutes, or until they are just fork-tender.

Transfer the green beans to a large serving bowl and toss them with the Garlic Spread & Dip and lemon juice until they are fully coated.

Top with the shredded Unexpected Cheddar Cheese and serve.

FRENCH ONION SLOW COOKER MASHED POTATOES

PREP TIME: 15 minutes
COOK TIME: 3 to 4 hours
SERVINGS: 12

You are going to fall head over heels for this recipe. Made with tender, creamy potatoes slow-cooked to perfection and infused with the rich, savory flavors of caramelized onions and Gruyère cheese, this side dish will have you dreaming of Parisian cafés and cozy, candlelit dinners. Whether you're looking for a comforting weeknight dinner or a showstopping holiday feast, these mashed potatoes are guaranteed to steal the spotlight and satisfy even the most demanding taste buds. *Bon appétit!*

¼ cup (57 g) unsalted butter

3 tbsp (45 ml) chicken broth

2 lb (905 g) Yukon Gold potatoes, peeled and cut into 1" (2.5-cm) cubes

½ cup (120 ml) whole milk, plus more if needed

Salt and freshly ground black pepper

½ cup (120 g) Caramelized Onion Dip

1 cup (113 g) shredded Gruyère cheese, plus more if needed

Finely chopped fresh chives, for garnish

Set your slow cooker to HIGH and place the butter and chicken broth in the slow cooker pot. Allow it to start melting while you chop your potatoes.

Add the potatoes and cover; cook for 3 to 4 hours on HIGH. The cook time will vary depending on the size you cut your potatoes. Cook until the potatoes are soft and easily mashed with a fork.

When the potatoes are soft, add the milk, plus salt and pepper to taste. Using an electric hand mixer, mash the potatoes directly in the slow cooker pot.

Then, fold in the Caramelized Onion Dip and Gruyère shredded cheese.

Add more milk if the texture is too thick. Taste, and add more Caramelized Onion Dip, if needed. Top the mashed potatoes with chives and serve.

NOTE: Try topping your mashed potatoes with fresh-made caramelized onions for more flavor!

BRUSCHETTA PASTA SALAD

PREP TIME: 5 minutes
COOK TIME: 15 minutes
SERVINGS: 5

Your taste buds are about to be singing an Italian opera! This salad is like a symphony of flavors with each bite. The Bruschetta Sauce, composed of juicy tomatoes, fresh basil and tangy balsamic vinegar, provides a perfectly harmonious dressing. Tossed with al dente pasta and drizzled with olive oil, this salad hits all the right notes. It's a true pasta-pella masterpiece!

1 (17.6-oz [500-g]) package Organic Italian Artisan Gigli Pasta

2 tbsp (30 ml) extra virgin olive oil

30 oz (850 g) Bruschetta Sauce

8 oz (115 g) Marinated Fresh Mozzarella Cheese balls, sliced in half

½ cup (20 g) chopped fresh basil

Cook the pasta according to the package instructions.

When the pasta has finished cooking, reserve ¼ cup (120 ml) of the pasta water, then drain and rinse the pasta with cool water.

Transfer the pasta to a large serving dish and toss with the olive oil, mix in the Bruschetta Sauce and some of the reserved pasta water to thin to your desired consistency, then top with the mozzarella balls and basil.

Serve cold, warm or at room temperature.

NOTES

- Scoop some of the herbs out of the marinated mozzarella container for extra flavor!
- Sometimes, I like to add Grilled Balsamic Vinegar & Rosemary Chicken to this pasta salad.

THINGS BETWEEN BREAD

We're normalizing sandwiches in this chapter, okay? They meet all the food groups and are so satisfying. Sandwiches can feature many different types of bread, such as sourdough, pita or even Ezekiel bread if you want to add even more nutrients! They can be filled with an abundance of vegetables, meat, cheese, spreads and herbs, among other ingredients. The possibilities are truly endless. They're great to serve for any meal and are perfect as a grab-and-go food if you are tight on time.

Some of the sandwiches in this section may be familiar to you, but with some twists to make them extra flavorful and unique. A traditional BLT is elevated with the addition of savory Garlic Spread & Dip (page 107), while a grilled cheese sandwich (page 112) is stuffed with bacon, apple butter and fresh apple for a sweet and salty contrast to oozing Gruyère cheese. Whatever your favorite sandwich is, you will surely find one to salivate over.

GARLICKY BLT

PREP TIME: 10 minutes
COOK TIME: 5 minutes
SERVINGS: 2

Looking for a BLT with a little extra oomph? Look no further than this garlicky twist on a classic favorite! The creamy Garlic Spread & Dip adds an unmatched garlicky savoriness that complements the sweet sun-ripened tomato, crisp lettuce and salty bacon, all nestled in between two toasted slices of sourdough bread.

¼ cup (56 g) Garlic Spread & Dip

4 slices sourdough bread

2 cups (150 g) butter lettuce

1 beefsteak tomato, sliced

6 slices bacon, cooked

Preheat the oven to 400°F (200°C). Evenly spread the Garlic Spread & Dip over one side of each piece of bread, then toast directly on the middle rack for 4 to 5 minutes, or to your liking.

Layer the lettuce, tomato and bacon over the spread on one slice of bread. Then place the remaining slice on top and cut in half. Repeat for the second sandwich and enjoy!

NOTE: Chopped butter lettuce is my favorite for this sandwich, but you can use whatever you like.

BRIE AND TURKEY SANDWICH

PREP TIME: 10 minutes

COOK TIME: 7 to 10 minutes

SERVINGS: 2

These oven-toasted sandwiches make for a scrumptious lunch at home or even a dinner with a salad and/or fries. They are filled with Fig Butter, oozy Brie, peppery arugula and cooked turkey, and served hot from the oven for a step up from the typical deli-style turkey sandwich. Mmmm, yum!

¼ cup (80 g) Fig Butter

4 slices sourdough bread

8 oz (225 g) Brie cheese, sliced thinly

1 (16-oz [454-g]) package Sliced Roast Turkey Breast

½ cup (10 g) baby arugula

Preheat the oven to 400°F (200°C).

Spread an even layer of Fig Butter on one side of each slice of bread.

Lay the sliced Brie on two of the slices. Place all four slices of bread, Brie side up, on a baking sheet in the oven and toast for 5 to 7 minutes, or until the cheese begins to melt and the bread starts to get crisp.

Remove the bread from the oven and place the turkey on top of the melted cheese. Place the bread back in the oven for 2 to 3 minutes to finish toasting the bread and to warm the turkey.

Arrange the arugula over the turkey and place the remaining slices of bread on top to make two sandwiches. Slice in half and enjoy!

GYRO PITA POCKETS

PREP TIME: 10 minutes
COOK TIME: 2 to 10 minutes
SERVINGS: 2

These easy pita pockets comprise just seven ingredients (yes, just seven) and can be whipped up in a matter of minutes. You can use any leftover tzatziki and cucumber you might have from making the Cool Cucumber Sandwich (page 116)!

1 (8-oz [227-g]) package Gyro Slices

2 pita breads

2 tbsp (30 ml) tzatziki

1 cup (75 g) shredded romaine lettuce

1 tomato, sliced

1 cucumber, sliced

¼ cup (40 g) thinly sliced red onion

Heat the Gyro Slices according to the package instructions.

Meanwhile, heat the pita breads over an open flame of a gas stove for 30 to 60 seconds per side, or in a 375°F (190°C) oven for 5 to 10 minutes.

Slice the pitas in half and spread a thin layer of tzatziki on the inside. Divide the Gyro Slices equally between each pita pocket, then add the romaine, tomato, cucumber and red onion.

APPLE BUTTER SHALLOT GRILLED CHEESE

PREP TIME: 10 minutes

COOK TIME: 17 to 23 minutes

SERVINGS: 2

This sandwich is like a cozy autumn day in every bite, with a gooey blend of nutty Brie and Gruyère cheese oozing between crispy slices of bread, slathered with rich apple butter and topped with crisp apple and bacon. It's for those who love a sweet and salty balance, and appreciate everything that a great grilled cheese has to offer!

4 slices bacon, sliced into ½" (1.3-cm) strips or cubes

1 tbsp (15 ml) olive oil

3 large shallots, diced

2 tbsp (30 ml) mayonnaise

4 slices sourdough bread

¼ cup (72 g) apple butter

4 oz (112 g) Brie cheese, sliced thinly

1 apple, sliced thinly

½ cup (58 g) shredded Gruyère cheese

1 tbsp (14 g) unsalted butter

Preheat the oven to 425°F (220°C) and line a baking sheet with foil. On the prepared pan, arrange the bacon in a single layer and bake for 15 to 20 minutes, or until crispy.

Meanwhile, in a medium-sized heavy-bottomed skillet, heat the olive oil over medium heat. Add the shallots and cook, tossing occasionally, for 5 to 6 minutes, or until they soften and begin to brown.

On a plate or cutting board, evenly spread a layer of mayonnaise over one side of each slice of bread. Flip the bread over so the non-mayonnaise sides face up. Evenly spread the apple butter on the upturned side of all four slices of bread. On two of the slices, over the apple butter, lay the sliced Brie in a single layer and top with the apple slices, shallots, bacon and Gruyère cheese.

Place the remaining two slices of bread, apple butter side down, on top to make two sandwiches.

In the same pan you used to cook the shallots, melt the butter over medium heat.

Place the sandwiches in the pan, mayonnaise side down, and cook for 2 to 3 minutes on each side, or until browned and crisp and the cheese is melted. Slice in half and serve hot.

NOTE: Leftover bacon can be used to make the Brussels Sprouts Flatbread (page 89) or the Bacon, Egg and Cheese Pastry Puffs (page 135).

CHILI CRISP GRILLED CHEESE

PREP TIME: 10 minutes
COOK TIME: 8 to 12 minutes
SERVINGS: 2

Grilled cheese was one of my favorite meals while growing up. I still crave it as an adult, but now I love to play with new flavors and make each one unique. This one is cheesy, fiery and a little sweet, so it checks all the boxes to make your taste buds sing! A touch of sweet honey and the heat of the Crunchy Chili Onion are unexpected additions that make this grilled cheese something to salivate for.

4 slices sourdough bread

2 tbsp (30 ml) mayonnaise

2 tbsp (36 g) Crunchy Chili Onion

⅔ cup (76 g) shredded Unexpected Cheddar Cheese

⅔ cup (77 g) shredded mozzarella cheese

2 tbsp (30 ml) honey

Unsalted butter, for cooking

On a plate or cutting board, lay out the bread slices and evenly spread one side of each with mayonnaise. Flip the bread slices over and evenly spread the other side with Crunchy Chili Onion. If you want it to be less spicy, spread the Crunchy Chili Onion on only one side of each slice instead of both.

Divide the Cheddar and mozzerella cheeses between two of the slices of bread, placing them atop the Crunchy Chili Onion.

Drizzle the honey evenly over the cheese.

Place the remaining two slices of bread, mayonnaise side up, on top to make two sandwiches.

In a medium-sized skillet, melt the butter over medium heat, then add the sandwiches. Cook for 4 to 6 minutes on each side, or until browned and crisp and the cheese is melted. Slice in half and serve hot.

COOL CUCUMBER SANDWICH

PREP TIME: 10 minutes
COOK TIME: 3 to 4 minutes
SERVINGS: 2

This elevated version of a cucumber sandwich is stuffed with caramelized shallots, crisp, cool cucumber, arugula and tzatziki. Trader Joe's tzatziki is truly exceptionally delicious because of its creamy texture, tangy flavor and perfect balance of garlic and dill. The refreshing combination of ingredients makes these sammies an exceptional choice for a picnic or poolside lunch on a hot summer day!

3 tbsp (43 g) unsalted butter

3 large shallots, diced finely

Coarse salt

4 slices Ezekiel bread

½ cup (10 g) baby arugula

2 tbsp (30 ml) extra virgin olive oil

2 tbsp (30 ml) tzatziki

1 cucumber, skin on, sliced thinly

Freshly ground black pepper

1 tbsp (4 g) finely chopped fresh dill

In a small skillet, heat the butter over medium heat. Add the shallots and a pinch of salt, and sauté, tossing occasionally, for 3 to 4 minutes, or until the shallots are translucent and start to caramelize.

Toast the bread to your liking while the shallots are cooking.

Meanwhile, in a small bowl, toss the baby arugula with the olive oil and a pinch of salt.

Let the bread cool, then spread an even layer of tzatziki on one side of all four slices of bread.

Layer the sautéed shallots, cucumber, pepper, dill and arugula over the tzatziki on half the bread slices. Place the remaining bread on top of each, tzatziki side down, and slice in half.

NOTE: You can slice the cucumber any way you like; I used a mandoline to make thin, long strips.

BOUJIE BOXED SOUPS

Ready to cozy up with a warm bowl of goodness that tastes like it's been simmering on the stove for hours? The souperheroes of this soup-er simple chapter are here for you! These recipes are made with boxed soups as the base with just a handful of fresh ingredients to elevate them to homemade status without all the fuss.

This chapter is for when you want your boxed soup to be more than a boxed soup, but you don't feel like making soup from scratch. With just a little bit of effort, you can enjoy a nourishing and delicious meal that will warm your soul and make you feel like a kitchen hero. My favorite is the Chicken Wonton Soup (page 122)!

TOMATO SOUP WITH "GRILLED CHEESE CROUTONS"

PREP TIME: 5 minutes
COOK TIME: 18 to 20 minutes
SERVINGS: 4

A big bowl of tomato soup and grilled cheese is so nostalgic. Trader Joe's has this delicious Outside-In Stuffed Gnocchi that reminds me of a grilled cheese because it's stuffed with mozzarella. Crisping them up in the oven and adding them to creamy tomato soup is an instant level up!

1 lb (455 g) Outside-In Stuffed Gnocchi

1 tbsp (15 ml) olive oil

12 oz (355 ml) Creamy Tomato Soup

¼ cup (10 g) finely chopped fresh basil, for garnish

Preheat the oven to 400°F (200°C). On a baking sheet, arrange the gnocchi in a single layer.

Toss the gnocchi with the olive oil and bake for 18 to 20 minutes, or until the bottoms start to crisp.

Meanwhile, in a medium-sized pot, heat the tomato soup over medium heat, stirring occasionally, for 10 to 12 minutes, or until it starts to bubble.

Divide the soup between four bowls and top with the cooked gnocchi and basil.

NOTES

- Try using Trader Joe's Cheese Tortellini in the tomato soup for a different take on this recipe!

- Adding spinach is an easy way to boost the nutrients in this delicious soup.

- Alternatively, you can make the gnocchi in an air fryer at 300°F (150°C) for 8 to 10 minutes or, in a skillet with 1 tablespoon of olive oil (15 ml) or butter (14 g), cook on each side for 3 to 5 minutes, or until golden brown.

CHICKEN WONTON SOUP

PREP TIME: 5 minutes
COOK TIME: 15 minutes
SERVINGS: 4

I threw this together one night when I didn't feel like cooking and it turned out *amazing*. I know it's going to be one of your new go-tos! It's so quick and easy, but tastes homemade. The best part is you can keep all these ingredients on hand, so you can enjoy this soup anytime!

12 oz (355 ml) Miso Ginger Broth

12 oz (340 g) Frozen Chicken Wontons

½ (13.4-oz [380-g]) package (2 individual packets) Squiggly Knife Cut Style Noodles

½ cup (27 g) thinly sliced green onions

1 to 2 tbsp (18–36 g) Crunchy Chili Onion (optional)

In a large soup pot over medium-high heat, bring the Miso Ginger Broth to a light boil.

Add the chicken wontons and cook for about 3 minutes, then add the noodles. Continue to cook, stirring occasionally, for 3 to 4 minutes, or until the noodles are just tender.

Remove the pot from the heat and stir in the green onions.

To serve, divide the soup and noodles among four bowls and enjoy! If you want to add a little heat to your soup, you can stir in a bit of Crunchy Chili Onion.

NOTE: I think this broth is pretty mild, so if you want to add more flavor, you can add a dash of soy sauce and some grated fresh ginger. I usually throw one or two Frozen Ginger Cubes into mine because I really love ginger!

CREAMY PORTOBELLO MUSHROOM SOUP

PREP TIME: 5 minutes
COOK TIME: 25 to 28 minutes
SERVINGS: 4

A creamy mushroom soup with sautéed mushrooms is a cozy and comforting meal that's perfect for any chilly day—and it can be yours in very little time by using prepared Trader Joe's Condensed Cream of Portabella Mushroom Soup as a base and doctoring it up with fresh aromatics and your choice of garnishes. The addition of sautéed onion and garlic takes the mushroom soup over the top and makes it taste like it's been simmering all day.

---

2 tbsp (28 g) unsalted butter

1 yellow onion, diced

2 Frozen Garlic Cubes

1 lb (455 g) cremini mushrooms, sliced thinly

¼ tsp kosher salt

11 oz (312 g) Condensed Cream of Portabella Mushroom Soup

3 cups (710 ml) vegetable broth

½ cup (120 ml) heavy cream

Optional garnishes: cream or olive oil for drizzling, chopped fresh parsley, croutons or toasted bread

In a large soup pot, melt the butter over medium-high heat.

Add the onion and garlic cubes, and sauté for 2 to 3 minutes, or until the onion begins to soften.

Lower the heat to medium. Add the cremini mushrooms and salt to the pot and sauté for 8 to 10 minutes, or until the mushrooms release their juices and become tender.

Mix in the cream of mushroom soup and vegetable broth, cover and bring the soup to a light boil, then lower the heat to medium-low and simmer, uncovered, for 15 minutes. In the last 2 minutes of cooking, stir in the heavy cream.

Working in batches, transfer the soup to a blender or use a stick blender right in the pot to blend until the soup is smooth.

Divide the soup among four bowls and drizzle and/or garnish with the toppings of your choice.

NOTES

- I love having the sliced mushrooms in the soup, and if you do, too, skip the blending step at the end.
- Sometimes, I like to add a variety of different mushrooms for a more interesting flavor.
- This soup can be made creamy or brothy. If you prefer a brothy soup, you can leave out the heavy cream.

CREAMY RAMEN TOMATO SOUP

PREP TIME: 5 minutes
COOK TIME: 16 to 21 minutes
SERVINGS: 2

A grilled cheese sandwich and tomato soup is one of my favorite combos, but sometimes I'm too lazy to even make a grilled cheese. Since eating tomato soup by itself isn't as fun, I added ramen to make it more interesting and fun to eat. It gives you the cozy feel-good feeling that comes from having a grilled cheese, while allowing you to use a pantry item that you can have on hand and don't have to worry about going bad.

1½ tsp (23 ml) olive oil

2 Frozen Garlic Cubes

2 large shallots, minced

¼ tsp red pepper flakes

1 (32-oz [946-ml]) package Tomato & Roasted Red Pepper Soup

4 Ramen Noodle Cups

½ cup (120 ml) half-and-half

½ cup (20 g) torn fresh basil

2 cups (65 g) packed baby spinach

Bring a large pot of water to a boil.

Meanwhile, in a large saucepan or a large, deep sauté pan, heat the olive oil over medium-high heat. Then, add the garlic cubes and cook, stirring occasionally, for about 1 minute. Add the shallots and red pepper flakes, and cook, stirring constantly, for 4 to 5 minutes, or until the shallots begin to caramelize.

Lower the heat to medium and pour in the Tomato & Roasted Red Pepper Soup. Continue to cook, stirring occasionally, for 8 to 10 minutes, or until the soup is completely heated through and beginning to simmer.

While the soup heats, empty the noodles from the ramen cups (discard the seasoning and oil packets) into the pot of boiling water and cook for 3 to 5 minutes, or until the noodles are al dente. Drain the noodles and rinse with cold water to keep them from cooking any longer.

Add the half-and-half to the saucepan of soup and stir. Then, add the basil and spinach. Heat for 2 to 3 minutes, or until the spinach has wilted, then add the cooked ramen noodles and heat for 1 to 2 more minutes.

Divide between two bowls and serve hot.

NOTES

- Alternatively, you can use the Trader Joe's Squiggly Knife Cut Style Noodles for this recipe in place of the ramen.

- In this recipe, do not use the seasoning packets or the oil from the ramen noodle cups.

MORNING MUNCHIES

I'm a savory girl all the way when it comes to breakfast foods, and that is reflected in my brunch recipes, which include Bacon, Egg and Cheese Pastry Puffs (page 135) which are hand pies perfect for breakfast on the go, and a Carnitas Potato Hash (page 139; I love this on a Sunday morning). I can get down with waffles and pancakes from time to time, but more often than not, I'm reaching for something savory. A sweet and savory combo can really win me over though, such as the Hot Honey Chicken and Waffles (page 132). Mmm, they are so good, with crisp-on-the-outside chicken tenders glazed in sweet and spicy hot honey along with golden waffles!

The recipes in this chapter are all very easy and take 30 minutes or less to make. Plus, each can stand on its own without the need to serve with other accompaniments.

PUMPKIN SPICE CHALLAH FRENCH TOAST

PREP TIME: 15 minutes
COOK TIME: 25 minutes
SERVINGS: 2

This cozy and comforting breakfast favorite is the perfect way to start your day during sweater weather. Thick slices of soft and fluffy challah bread are soaked in a sweet pumpkin-spiced custard, then cooked to golden perfection. Top it all off with a dollop of whipped cream and a sprinkle of cinnamon. Each bite is like a cozy hug in your mouth!

6 large eggs

1 cup (240 ml) whole milk

¾ cup (184 g) pure pumpkin purée

3 tbsp (45 g) packed light brown sugar

2 tsp (10 ml) vanilla extract

1 tbsp (10 g) pumpkin pie spice

1 tsp ground cinnamon

¼ tsp kosher salt

1 loaf challah, sliced into 1½" (4-cm)-thick slices

Unsalted butter, for cooking

Optional toppings: whipped cream, ground cinnamon, powdered sugar, butter and/or pure maple syrup

In a large bowl, whisk together the eggs, milk, pumpkin purée, brown sugar, vanilla, pumpkin pie spice, cinnamon and salt.

Dip the bread into the egg mixture and lightly press down to coat both sides.

In a large nonstick skillet, melt the butter over medium heat. When the butter has melted, transfer two of the bread slices to the skillet and cook for 3 to 4 minutes on each side, or until golden brown. Repeat with the rest of the bread slices.

Serve warm with whipped cream, ground cinnamon, powdered sugar, butter and/or maple syrup, if desired.

NOTE: You can use Trader Joe's sliced brioche bread instead of challah if you'd prefer.

HOT HONEY CHICKEN AND WAFFLES

PREP TIME: 5 minutes
COOK TIME: 20 to 25 minutes
SERVINGS: 4

This super easy chicken and waffles recipe is made with just three ingredients, so it's easy to prepare as a special brunch dish for your family on the weekend. Almost everything comes from the frozen aisle in Trader Joe's, so you can have these items on hand anytime! The hot honey will add some sweet, savory and spicy notes, making these chicken and waffles truly addictive.

4 Frozen Breaded Chicken Tenderloin Breasts

4 Frozen Multi Grain Toaster Waffles

Hot honey, for drizzling

Preheat the oven to 425°F (220°C).

On a baking sheet, arrange the chicken tenders in a single layer, then bake for 20 to 25 minutes, or until fully heated through and crispy.

Meanwhile, toast the waffles to your liking.

Top each waffle with a chicken tender and drizzle with hot honey.

NOTE: I love making the chicken tenders in an air fryer! I cook them at 350°F (180°C) for 12 to 15 minutes.

BACON, EGG AND CHEESE PASTRY PUFFS

PREP TIME: 15 minutes
COOK TIME: 30 to 35 minutes
SERVINGS: Makes 12 pastry puffs

These little pastry puffs are the ultimate breakfast indulgence! Fluffy and buttery puffs are loaded with crispy bacon, velvety eggs and ooey-gooey melted Unexpected Cheddar Cheese. The best part? You can have it on the go! These handheld pastries are perfect for breakfast on the run or for a brunch party with friends. So, grab one (or two) of these savory delights and let the flavors dance in your mouth!

---

6 large eggs

¼ cup (60 ml) milk

Salt and freshly ground black pepper

1 tbsp (15 ml) olive oil

2 tbsp (15 g) all-purpose flour, for dusting

2 sheets puff pastry

4 strips bacon, cooked and diced finely

½ cup shredded Unexpected Cheddar Cheese

In a medium-sized bowl, beat together the eggs and milk, then season with salt and pepper. Set ½ cup (120 ml) of this mixture aside to use as an egg wash.

In a medium-sized nonstick skillet, heat the olive oil over medium heat. When hot, add the eggs to the pan and use a spatula to scramble them.

When the eggs have finished cooking, remove from the heat and allow them to cool completely before assembling the pastry puffs.

Preheat the oven to 400°F (200°C) while you prepare the pastries. Line a baking sheet with parchment paper.

Onto a clean surface, sprinkle a light dusting of flour. Place the puff pastry over the flour and cut each into six 4 x 5-inch (10 x 13-cm) rectangles. Use a fork to gently poke holes down into the center of the dough, then brush the edges of the pastry squares with the reserved egg wash.

Fill the center of the pastries with about 1 tablespoon (14 g) of the scrambled eggs, 1 tablespoon (5 g) diced cooked bacon and 1 tablespoon (about 8 g) of shredded cheese.

Transfer the pastries to the prepared baking sheet. Bake for 20 to 25 minutes, or until they are golden brown. I like mine extra crispy! Remove from the oven and let the pastry puffs cool for 5 minutes before serving.

NOTE: To reheat, place the pastry puffs in a 350°F (180°C) oven for 8 to 10 minutes.

EVERYTHING BUT THE BAGEL SALMON TARTE

PREP TIME: 15 minutes
COOK TIME: 20 to 25 minutes
SERVINGS: 4

Think traditional bagel and lox but with buttery, crisp pastry instead of the bagel, and whipped cream cheese for an extra-smooth and heavenly bite! The combo of ingredients is beyond perfection with smoky salmon, briny capers, pickled onions, fresh dill and a good sprinkle of Everything but the Bagel Sesame Seasoning Blend. This twist on a classic will be sure to knock any bagel lover's socks off.

1 small red onion, sliced very thinly

1 cup (240 ml) white vinegar

1 cup (240 ml) water

2 tbsp (26 g) sugar

1 sheet puff pastry

1 large egg, beaten lightly, for egg wash

3 tbsp (36 g) Everything but the Bagel Sesame Seasoning Blend, plus more for garnish

⅔ cup (133 g) whipped cream cheese

1 (4-oz [113-g]) package Everything but the Bagel Seasoned Smoked Salmon

3 tbsp (12 g) chopped fresh dill

3 tbsp (26 g) drained capers

Fresh lemon juice (optional)

Preheat the oven to 425°F (220°C) and line a baking sheet with parchment paper.

Pickle the red onion: Place the onion slices in a heatproof glass jar. In a medium-sized saucepan, heat the vinegar, water and sugar over medium heat. Stir until the sugar dissolves, about 1 minute. Pour the vinegar mixture over the onion and set aside to cool to room temperature.

Gently roll out the puff pastry with a rolling pin and place it on the prepared baking sheet. Use a fork to poke holes all over, then brush a thin layer of egg wash over the entire pastry.

Cover the border of the pastry with everything bagel seasoning and bake the puff pastry for 20 to 25 minutes, or until golden brown and puffy. Every 3 to 5 minutes, remove the pastry from the oven and flatten the center with a fork or the back of a spoon.

Remove from the oven and let the pastry come to room temperature before carefully spreading the cream cheese over the tart. If a few pieces flake from the bottom, that's okay! This is why we use whipped cream cheese vs regular cream cheese. It's much lighter!

Layer the smoked salmon on top of the cream cheese and garnish with pickled onion, fresh dill, capers and the everything bagel seasoning. If you like, add a squeeze of fresh lemon juice as well! Slice into squares and serve.

CARNITAS POTATO HASH

PREP TIME: 10 minutes
COOK TIME: 30 to 38 minutes
SERVINGS: 4

Start your day with a little fiesta in your mouth with this colorful hash, made up of juicy pork Traditional Carnitas and cubed sweet potatoes that are cooked until crispy and then topped with fried eggs and cilantro before serving.

2 medium-sized sweet potatoes, cut into ½" (1.3-cm) cubes

2 tbsp (30 ml) olive oil

¼ tsp kosher salt

¼ tsp freshly ground black pepper

1½ tsp (4 g) paprika

1 (12-oz [340-g]) package Traditional Carnitas

Juice of 1 orange; zest optional

4 large eggs

¼ cup (4 g) fresh cilantro, chopped

Preheat the oven to 450°F (230°C). Place the sweet potatoes on a rimmed baking sheet and drizzle with the olive oil. Then, sprinkle them with the salt, pepper and paprika, and toss to coat them with the seasonings. Bake for 10 minutes, then toss and bake for 10 to 15 more minutes, or until the edges of the sweet potatoes start to brown.

Meanwhile, prepare the carnitas by transferring them from the package to a microwave-safe plate. Microwave on HIGH for 3 minutes. Then, shred the carnitas with two forks.

Heat a 12-inch (30-cm) cast-iron skillet over medium-high heat. Add the shredded carnitas to the pan and cook, tossing occasionally, for 6 to 8 minutes, or until they start to get crispy.

When the carnitas are crispy, add the orange juice and cook for about 30 more seconds. You can add some orange zest here, too, if you like!

When the potatoes have finished roasting, add them to the skillet with the carnitas and give them a good toss to mix everything together. Lower the heat to medium-low. Crack the eggs into the skillet and cook, covered, for 4 to 5 minutes, or until the white parts set.

When the eggs have finished cooking, remove the pan from the heat. Garnish with cilantro before serving.

DECADENT DELIGHTS

Sweet treats are essential in life, even for us savory people. But for us savory people, dessert isn't often our favorite thing to make. So, we have this little chapter full of nonintimidating desserts that are sure to satisfy even the sweetest of sweet tooths.

Here, you'll find an iteration of one of my favorite childhood desserts, a play on my grandmother's banana cream pie (Banana Cream Pie Cups [page 147]). All the grandkids used to fight over the biggest slice of pie—if only we had these individual pie cups back then! All my cookie dough lovers will adore the Edible Cookie Butter Cookie Dough (page 151) as well, which has the bonus of chunks of Trader Joe's cookies for decadent flavor and texture.

S'MORES BARS

PREP TIME: 10 minutes
COOK TIME: 40 minutes
SERVINGS: 12 bars

The wondrous ingredients of graham crackers, marshmallows and chocolate bars combine to allow you to have this traditional campfire treat without even having to set foot outdoors. Who doesn't love the taste of oozing chocolate and sweet, pillowy marshmallows?

¾ cup (170 g) plus 1 tbsp (14 g) unsalted butter, melted, for greasing

30 graham crackers, crushed finely, divided

¼ tsp kosher salt

4 cups (200 g) mini marshmallows, divided

10 oz (280 g) milk chocolate bars

Preheat the oven to 350°F (180°C) and grease a 9-inch (23-cm) square baking dish with the tablespoon (14 g) of melted butter.

In a large bowl, combine the graham cracker crumbs, reserving ¼ cup (23 g) of the crumbs for later use, with the remaining ¾ cup (170 g) of butter and salt. Press the mixture into an even layer, then bake for 20 minutes.

Top evenly with 2 cups (100 g) of the mini marshmallows and bake for 10 more minutes. Remove from the oven and allow to cool for 5 minutes to let the marshmallows deflate.

Add the chocolate bars in an even layer, then top evenly with the remaining 2 cups (100 g) of marshmallows. Sprinkle with the reserved graham cracker crumbs. Bake for 10 more minutes.

Remove from the oven and let the s'mores bars cool (this may take several hours) before slicing, or else they will break apart.

NOTES

- Use a food processor or blender to make the graham cracker crumbs; you want them to be very, very fine.

- The easiest way to cut the bars is to wait until they have completely cooled and the chocolate has solidified, then use a metal spatula to lift the entire thing out of the pan and transfer it to a cutting board for slicing.

- Get creative with your chocolate and mix-ins! You can add crushed chocolate-covered pretzels, or any of the fun flavored chocolates from Trader Joe's.

- I used two 3.17-ounce (90-g) boxes of the Trader Joe's Mini Milk Chocolate Bars.

HEALTHY-ER PEACHES & CREAM

PREP TIME: 5 minutes
COOK TIME: 0 minutes
SERVINGS: 2

Rather than using whipped cream, this peaches and cream recipe uses Greek yogurt for a slightly healthier twist on the traditional dessert. However, you likely won't miss the cream, as Greek yogurt has a thick creaminess to it and a much more complex flavor that is wonderful with sweet peaches and the pronounced chocolatiness of dark chocolate chips.

6 Yellow Cling Peach Halves in White Grape Juice

½ cup (115 g) Vanilla Bean Greek Yogurt

¼ cup (60 g) dark chocolate chips

Divide and layer the peach halves, Greek yogurt and chocolate chips equally between two glasses or bowls.

BANANA CREAM PIE CUPS

PREP TIME: 10 minutes
COOK TIME: 15 minutes
SERVINGS: 4

These banana cream pie cups are the perfect treat when you're craving something sweet. They're quick and easy to make, taking just about 25 minutes from start to finish. The best part? You can assemble them in cute stemless wineglasses or Mason jars to make them even more fun to eat! They're a great way to indulge in the classic flavors of banana cream pie, all in one little cup.

20 Old Fashioned Cinnamon Grahams

¼ cup (50 g) sugar

¼ tsp kosher salt

6 tbsp (85 g) unsalted butter, melted

¼ cup (60 ml) caramel sauce

3 bananas, sliced thinly

¾ cup (180 g) dark chocolate chips

Whipped cream

Preheat the oven to 350°F (180°C).

Place the graham crackers in a food processor and pulse on HIGH until they are ground into fine crumbs.

In a medium-sized bowl, combine the graham cracker crumbs, sugar and salt. Then, pour in the melted butter and mix with a spatula until fully combined.

Arrange the graham cracker mixture in an even layer, about ½ inch (1.3 cm) thick, on a baking sheet and bake for 15 minutes. If there are any clumps, break them up with a fork.

Place two spoonfuls of the graham cracker crumbs in each serving cup, then add 1 tablespoon (15 ml) of caramel sauce. Layer on the sliced bananas, chocolate chips, whipped cream and more graham cracker crumbs until the cups are full.

PEANUT BUTTER CHOCOLATE DATES

PREP TIME: 10 minutes
COOK TIME: 0 minutes
SERVINGS: 25 dates

These stuffed dates are great sweet little bites when you need to satisfy a sweet tooth fast but want something a little healthy, too. I love to keep these in the freezer to eat before going to the gym, or as an afternoon snack or a healthier dessert. They are just so satisfying with the slight chewiness of the dates, the crunchiness and creaminess of the peanut butter and the hint of flaky salt.

1 (12-oz [340-g]) package Organic Pitted Medjool Dates (about 25 dates)

½ cup (128 g) Unsalted Crunchy Peanut Butter

10 oz (280 g) dark chocolate chips

¼ cup (55 g) coconut oil

Flaky sea salt, for topping

Open the dates and stuff each with about 1½ teaspoons (8 g) of peanut butter.

In a medium-sized bowl, combine the chocolate chips and coconut oil. Microwave on HIGH in 30-second increments, stirring in between, until the chocolate has melted completely.

Dip the dates into the melted chocolate and toss to fully coat them.

Lay the dates on a baking sheet or a plate and sprinkle with sea salt. Depending on how quickly you're working, you may want to sprinkle with the salt right after dipping the dates in chocolate, because you'll want to add it before the chocolate sets, so it sticks.

Place the dates in the freezer and freeze until you're ready to eat.

EDIBLE COOKIE BUTTER COOKIE DOUGH

PREP TIME: 10 minutes
COOK TIME: 0 minutes
SERVINGS: 4

This is the ultimate dessert for anyone who loves cookie dough and cookie butter. With a rich and creamy texture, this cookie dough is packed with salty, chocolaty pretzel chunks and swirls of cookie butter. This mixture is perfectly safe to consume as it doesn't contain any eggs or raw flour, so go ahead, grab a bowl and enter a blissful state with this decadent cookie dough.

½ cup (115 g) light brown sugar

¼ cup (50 g) granulated sugar

½ cup (114 g) unsalted butter, at room temperature

2 tsp (10 ml) vanilla extract

⅓ tsp salt

¾ cup (75 g) almond flour

½ cup (32 g) roughly chopped Dark Chocolate Covered Mini Pretzels

¼ cup (60 g) Speculoos Cookie Butter

Into a large bowl, sift the sugars together, then add the butter and mix with an electric hand mixer until soft and fluffy. Then, mix in the vanilla and salt. Sift in the almond flour and continue to mix until all ingredients are fully combined.

Fold in the pretzels and cookie butter, using a spatula.

Divide among four bowls and serve, or store in a glass jar in the refrigerator for 3 to 4 days.

NOTE: If you don't have almond flour, you can replace it with another flour, such as whole wheat or all-purpose; just make sure you heat treat it in the oven first so it's safe to eat. To heat treat the flour, bake it on a baking sheet at 350°F (180°C) for 5 to 10 minutes, or until it's reached 160°F (71°C).

ACKNOWLEDGMENTS

MOM

To my mom, thank you for opening my eyes to new cuisines throughout my childhood. Whether it was through traveling or dining at restaurants, you always made sure I experienced some of the best food and tried new things. When we weren't dining out, I always had a delicious home-cooked meal for dinner, thanks to you. Most importantly, thank you for passing on your extremely strong work ethic. I couldn't do this job without it!

DAD

To my dad, thank you for teaching me your intuitive style of cooking, sharing the flavors of all the herbs in the garden when I was a kid so I knew what everything smelled and tasted like and for always including me in the kitchen at dinnertime. I've learned to have a great appreciation for everything from coffee to fine wine to challenging my palate to always try new things.

Thank you both for supporting me through the good and the bad. And a special thank-you for teaching me the importance of eating together as a family. No matter how small our family might have been, we always had dinner together. Even if it was just me and my mom or me and my dad. I never ate alone and I've carried that with me as an adult. In my house now, we always eat together!

JZ EATS SUPPORTERS

To all the fans and supporters of JZ Eats, a big thank-you for being here and continuing to support me and my business. All your recipe ratings, blog post comments, engagement on social media and kind messages make this all possible. You all are the best!

PUBLISHER

To Marissa, Meg and the rest of the Page Street Publishing team, thank you for all your help in bringing this book to life!

PHOTOGRAPHER

To Katerina, thank you for your exceptional dedication and outstanding craftsmanship in capturing the breathtaking photos for this book. Your hard work has brought these pages to life, and I am sincerely grateful for your remarkable talent and unwavering commitment.

TRADER JOE'S

A special thank-you to my local Trader Joe's employees for always taking my phone calls to ask about products I wanted to use in my book! They have some of the best and most enjoyable employees and it's a big part of the reason I love shopping there.

ABOUT THE AUTHOR

JORDAN is a talented recipe developer and food photographer with a lifelong love for food. Her culinary creativity has been featured in various media outlets, such as BuzzFeed, *People* magazine, *Good Morning America*, Baltimore Style magazine, *Baltimore Sun*, Yahoo! and various others.

From a young age, Jordan has always had a passion for cooking and a flair for the artistic, which is reflected in her food blog and cookbook.

Originally from Maryland, Jordan now resides in northern New Jersey with her husband and their two cats, Luna and Layla. When she's not in the kitchen, Jordan enjoys staying active and has participated in a triathlon, half marathon and various other races. She also loves exploring new restaurants, traveling and spending time with friends.

Jordan's recipes and culinary creations can be found on her website, www.jz-eats.com, as well as on her popular social media accounts on Instagram and TikTok, where she goes by the handle @jzeats.

INDEX

155